CULTURES OF THE WORLD

Dominican Republic

Cavendish
Square

New York

Published in 2016 by Cavendish Square Publishing, LLC
243 5th Avenue, Suite 136, New York, NY 10016
Copyright © 2016 by Cavendish Square Publishing, LLC
Third Edition

This publication represents the opinions and views of the author based on his or her personal experience, knowledge, and research. The information in this book serves as a general guide only. The author and publisher have used their best efforts in preparing this book and disclaim liability rising directly or indirectly from the use and application of this book.

CPSIA Compliance Information: Batch #CW16CSQ

All websites were available and accurate when this book was sent to press.

Cataloging-in-Publication Data

Names: Foley, Erin, 1967-.
Title: Dominican Republic / Erin Foley, Leslie Jermyn, and Debbie Nevins.
Description: New York: Cavendish Square Publishing, 2016 | Series: Cultures of the world | Includes index.
Identifiers: ISBN 9781502608048 (library bound) | ISBN 9781502608055 (ebook)
Subjects: LCSH: Dominican Republic—Juvenile literature.
Classification: LCC F1934.2 F65 2016 | DDC 972.93--dc23

Writers, Erin Foley, Leslie Jermyn, second edition; Charles Piddock, Debbie Nevins, third edition
Editor, third edition: Debbie Nevins
Art Director, third edition: Jeffrey Talbot
Designer, third edition: Jessica Nevins
Production Manager, third edition Jennifer Ryder-Talbot
Cover Picture Researcher: Stephanie Flecha
Picture Researcher, third edition: Jessica Nevins

PICTURE CREDITS

The photographs in this book are used with the permission of: Danita Delimont/Gallo Images/Getty Images, cover; mandritoiu/Shutterstock.com, 1; Chad Gordon Higgins/Shutterstock.com, 3; Leanne Walker/Lonely Planet Images/Getty Images, 5; Kovnir Andrii/Shutterstock.com, 6; Anna Jedynak/Shutterstock.com, 7; ERIKA SANTELICES/AFP/Getty Images, 8; ERIKA SANTELICES/AFP/Getty Images, 9; Artindo/Shutterstock.com, 10; Ramona Heim/Shutterstock.com, 11; Jeanette Dietl/Shutterstock.com, 12; Reinhard Dirscherl/ullstein bild via Getty Images, 13; © Hemis/Alamy, 14; ERIKA SANTELICES/AFP/Getty Images, 15; watthanachai/Shutterstock.com, 16; Alvin Padayachee/File:Chupacabra padayachee.jpg/Wikimedia Commons, 17; Enrique Ramos/Shutterstock.com, 18; Ulora/Shutterstock.com, 19; © Hackenberg-Photo-Cologne/Alamy, 20; Artefficient/Shutterstock.com, 21; Papa Bravo/Shutterstock.com, 22; Travel Ink/Gallo Images/Getty Images, 24; Reinhard Dirscherl/ullstein bild via Getty Images, 25; DEA PICTURE LIBRARY/Getty Images, 27; Hulton Archive/Getty Images, 28; Education Images/UIG via Getty Images, 29; Frank Dominguez/File:Hereaux2.gif/Wikimedia Commons, 30; Dominican newspaper El Caribe, 1951/File:Magloire Trujillo 1951.jpg/Wikimedia Commons, 32; Hugo van Gelderen/Anefo/File:Juan Bosch (1963).jpg/Wikimedia Commons, 33; ullstein bild/ullstein bild via Getty Images, 34; Robert W. Kelley/The LIFE Picture Collection/Getty Images, 35; TIMOTHY CLARY/AFP/Getty Images, 36; ERIKA SANTELICES/AFP/Getty Images, 37; Gary Blakeley/Shutterstock.com, 38; JUAN BARRETO/AFP/Getty Images, 40; ERIKA SANTELICES/AFP/Getty Images, 42; Pablo Matos/LatinContent/Getty Images, 43; ERIKA SANTELICES/AFP/Getty Images, 44; Valentin Valkov/Shutterstock.com, 46; Lars Christensen/Shutterstock.com, 48; SHCHERBAKOV SERGII/Shutterstock.com, 49; tandemich/Shutterstock.com, 50; Kovnir Andrii/Shutterstock.com, 51; Rob Lavinsky/iRocks.com (http://www.irocks.com/)/File:Falcondoite-Willemseite-215137.jpg/Wikimedia Commons, 52; Eye Ubiquitous/UIG via Getty Images, 53; Robert Nickelsberg/Getty Images, 54; Maciej Czekajewski/Shutterstock.com, 55; Ethan Daniels/Shutterstock.com, 56; Dikoz/Shutterstock.com, 58; Sean Pavone/Shutterstock.com, 59; Ethan Daniels/Shutterstock.com, 60; Goran Bogicevic/Shutterstock.com, 62; Danny Alvarez/Shutterstock.com, 64; ERIKA SANTELICES/AFP/Getty Images, 65; Steffen Thalemann/The Image Bank/Getty Images, 67; a katz/Shutterstock.com, 68; Spencer Platt/Getty Images, 69; Klemen Misic/Shutterstock.com, 70; Klemen Misic/Shutterstock.com, 71; Glenn Losack MD/Moment/Moment Editorial/Getty Images, 72; ERIKA SANTELICES/AFP/Getty Images, 73; Javier Teniente/Cover/Getty Images, 74; Hans Neleman/The Image Bank/Getty Images, 75; ERIKA SANTELICES/AFP/Getty Images, 77; ERIKA SANTELICES/AFP/Getty Images, 79; dean bertoncelj/Shutterstock.com, 80; Brigitte MERLE/Photononstop/Getty Images, 81; Marvin del Cid/Moment Open/Getty Images, 83; Maciej Czekajewski/Shutterstock.com, 84; Maremagnum/Photolibrary/Getty images, 86; VINCENZO PINTO/AFP/Getty Images, 87; ERIKA SANTELICES/AFP/Getty Images, 88; Bildagentur Zoonar GmbH/Shutterstock.com, 89; Dallas Stribley/Lonely Planet Images/Getty Images, 90; Alfredo Maiquez/Lonely Planet Images/Getty Images, 92; Baur/ullstein bild via Getty Images, 94; ERIKA SANTELICES/AFP/Getty Images, 95; Chris Mellor/Lonely Planet Images/Getty Images, 98; Architect of the Capitol/File:Flickr-USCapitol-Bartholomé de Las Casas.jpg/Wikimedia Commons, 100; Alex Wong/Getty Images, 101; Salim October/Shutterstock.com, 102; Baur/ullstein bild via Getty Images, 105; DEA/A.RIZZI/De Agostini/Getty Images, 106; Peter Bischoff/Getty Images, 107; Hans Neleman/The Image Bank/Getty Images, 108; GUIZIOU Franck/hemis.fr/Getty Images, 110; Michael Hanson/National Geographic/Getty Images, 112; ERIKA SANTELICES/AFP/Getty Images, 114; Santiago Vidal/LatinContent/Getty Images, 115; ERIKA SANTELICES/AFP/Getty Images, 117; ERIKA SANTELICES/AFP/Getty Images, 118; Danny Alvarez/Shutterstock.com, 119; MIGUEL GARCIA SAAVEDRA/Shutterstock.com, 120; Maria Bobrova/Shutterstock.com, 121; chriss73/Shutterstock.com, 122; bonchan/Shutterstock.com, 123; Matt Henry Gunther/The Image Bank/Getty Images, 124 rj lerich/Shutterstock.com, 125; pixshots/Shutterstock.com, 126; exoticartz/Shutterstock.com, 127; ERIKA SANTELICES/AFP/Getty Images, 128; govindji/Shutterstock.com, 130; Margaret M Stewart/Shutterstock.com, 131.

PRECEDING PAGE

An old fishing boat is pulled up on a beach in Cayo Levantado, Dominican Republic.

Printed in the United States of America

CONTENTS

DOMINICAN REPUBLIC TODAY

TO MANY, THE IMAGE OF THE DOMINICAN REPUBLIC TODAY IS a tropical "Wish You Were Here" postcard come to life—a place of warm breezes, swaying palm trees, musical Caribbean rhythms, and plentiful food from an ever-sunny turquoise sea.

At least that's what travel agents want to sell. No be sure, the Dominican Republic today is a tourist mecca. Hotels, restaurants, and lavish resorts crowd the country's beaches. Visitors from New York, Paris, London, and other cities fly into the nation's capital of Santo Domingo, then on to any number of resorts, enjoy the easy and colorful Dominican lifestyle, then fly home with memories of their own tropical paradise.

In 2015, the Dominican Republic remains the most popular tourist destination in the Caribbean and, with the construction of lavish mega-resorts like Cap Cana, San Souci Port in Santo Domingo, and the Moon Palace Resort in Punta Cana, the Dominican Republic is likely to stay Number One for years to come.

The country's booming tourist industry, however, is only part of story of the Dominican Republic today. Some of the other parts don't fit so nicely into a travel brochure.

A picture-postcard-worthy beach in the Dominican Republic looks like paradise.

The economic conditions in the Dominican Republic today are better for the vast majority of Dominicans than ever before. Average income has grown dramatically and more people have jobs than ever before. Still, too many Dominicans remain trapped in poverty. Approximately one-fifth of the nation's ten million people live in rural poverty in what even experts describe as "shacks" without access to running water, proper sanitation, and electricity. The same percentage of the population struggles to make a living on less than the equivalent of two US dollars a day. In a country that is home to hundreds of luxury tourist resorts and fine restaurants, one in five Dominicans remains chronically hungry and undernourished—despite the fact that the Dominican economy has been steadily growing since 1996.

Dominican poverty also has a young face. While one in five Dominicans lives in poverty, the figure among children under eighteen is one in two. According to a 2013 United Nations report, half of the children in the Dominican Republic struggle daily to get enough food, access to safe drinking water, and adequate housing. According to UNICEF, roughly 578,000 Dominican children under the age of fifteen are without adult care. Around 20 percent of them are orphans, many because their parents died from AIDS. Many of these children end up in the street, having given up school and forced to work.

The Dominican Republic Child Labor Survey indicates that roughly 15 percent of all children age five to fourteen are engaged in labor activities. As soon as they stop going to school, their lives are often marked by a vicious cycle of drugs, crime, and violence. Approximately 17,000 Dominican children who take part in the labor force do so without attending school. The percentage is particularly high for boys and for children who live in rural areas. Many of these children end up in the streets where they face a life under precarious circumstances. The highest incidence of extreme poverty in the Dominican Republic today occurs along the Dominican-Haiti border particularly in the mountainous areas, but also in the lower valleys where there is a high concentration of slums, called *bateyes* (bah-TAY-ays).

The persistence of such rural poverty in the Dominican Republic is the result of several factors, including years of the Dominican government giving priority in spending and development to the tourist industry. As a result, government investment in social and productive development in rural areas is limited.

Low agricultural productivity remains a major cause of rural poverty in the Dominican Republic in 2015. Although modern methods of farming to increase crop yields are available, farmers don't have the money to implement them. However, the profile of agriculture is changing, and groups of small-

Away from the tourist resorts, the life of ordinary Dominicans looks much like this.

Supporters of Dominican nationalist movements demonstrate in support of denying citizenship to thousands of Dominicans of Haitian descent. The sign reads, "Illegal Haitians get out of Dominican Republic."

scale farmers are reaping the benefits of improved technologies to increase the production of vegetable export crops as a source of added income.

On September 23, 2014, the highest court in the Dominican Republic, the Constitutional Tribunal, opened an old wound with a highly controversial legal decision. The court proclaimed that any Dominicans descended from undocumented Haitians going back to 1929 are to be stripped of their Dominican citizenship. The ruling affects an estimated 250,000 Dominicans of Haitian descent who are now legally without a country. While African blood circulates in many Dominicans, Haitians are directly descended from African slaves and have darker skin than most Dominicans, leading to charges of racism aimed at the Dominican government. Haitians in the Dominican Republic also are the poorest segment of the Dominican population.

The United Nations human rights office warned Dominican authorities of the dangers of implementing the new order.

"We are extremely concerned that a ruling of the Dominican Republic Constitutional Court may deprive tens of thousands of people of nationality, virtually all of them of Haitian descent, and have a very negative impact on their other rights," a statement by the office of the High Commissioner for Human Rights said.

Some are calling decision of the court has been called the latest manifestation of "anti-Haitianismo," a powerful anti-Haitian force in the Dominican Republic going back centuries. It involves money, race, ethnic identity, and a bitter history between the Dominican Republic and Haiti, the two nations that share the island of Hispaniola. The Dominican Republic's population today is 73 percent racially mixed, 16 percent white, and 11 percent black. Ethnic immigrant groups in the country include many Lebanese, Syrians, and Palestinians.

Many Dominicans strongly identify with the European ethnic part of their background, and reject the African part. Haitians, in contrast, are overwhelmingly black.

The Dominican Republic today is not a rich country, but it is a lot better off now than it was even ten years ago, and it is many times wealthier than Haiti. In terms of per capita GDP, the Dominican Republic is about six times richer than Haiti. So thousands of Haitians go to the Dominican Republic to find work. Haitians and their descendants may make up as many as one in ten of the Dominican Republic's population.

The Dominican government in Santo Domingo strongly denies charges of racism in its policies. But in 2007, a report prepared for the United Nations Office for the High Commissioner for Human Rights described what it called a "profound and entrenched problem of racism and discrimination in Dominican society, generally affecting blacks and particularly such groups as black Dominicans, Dominicans of Haitian descent, and Haitians."

Haitians demonstrate with signs reading, "I am Dominican like you," and "We are not foreigners."

According to official figure released in May 2014, there were at least 450,000 Haitian immigrants living in the Dominican Republic, most of them with resident permits. A 2010 constitutional reform had placed these people in an illegal status and barred them or their children from becoming Dominican citizens.

Human rights groups have warned that the decision could leave tens of thousands of people of Haitian descent stateless. But the Dominican Republic says it is trying to "regularize" the status of undocumented immigrants to its country.

Dominican President Danilo Medina, who denies any charges of racism or unfairness, said he would refuse to back down under pressure from human rights groups.

By July 2015, thousands of people of Haitian descent didn't wait to see if they would be forcibly removed from the Dominican Republic. They went back to Haiti. The Dominican government says that by that date nearly 40,000 had left.

GEOGRAPHY

The Dominican flag marks the position of the country on the island of Hispaniola and in the Caribbean.

1

THE DOMINICAN REPUBLIC OCCUPIES approximately two-thirds of the island of Hispaniola, the second largest island, after Cuba, in the West Indies. Haiti occupies the remaining western one-third of the island.

The Dominican Republic covers an area of 18,680 square miles (48,380 square kilometers), slightly larger than the combined square miles of Vermont and New Hampshire. It has a coastline of 800 miles (1,288 km), washed by the Atlantic Ocean on its north and the Caribbean Sea on its south.

Waves splash on a rocky coast of the Dominican Republic.

When Christopher Columbus landed on the island in 1492, he named it *La Isla Española.* Over time, that became anglicized to Hispaniola.

A mountainous landscape on the island country is lush and green.

The Dominican Republic has a great geographical diversity concentrated in a small area. The country's terrain includes mountain ranges, semi-desert lowlands, fertile valleys, tropical rain forests, wide beaches, rivers, and even a saltwater lake.

REGIONS

Four mountain ranges divide the Dominican Republic into northern, central, and southwestern regions. The main mountain range is the Cordillera Central, which forms the backbone of the country, with smaller mountain ranges on either side.

NORTHERN REGION The Dominican Republic's Atlantic coastal plain extends between the cities of Monte Cristi and Nagua. The Cordillera Septentrional, the range farthest north, rises from this plain with peaks around 3,280 feet (1,000 m) high.

The densely populated farmland of the Cibao Valley lies south of the Cordillera Septentrional. The country's second-largest city, Santiago, is located in the valley and is its commercial center. East of Santiago, the valley is called the Vega Real, or Royal Plain, where the land is fertile and suitable for the cultivation of crops such as coffee, corn, and tobacco.

CENTRAL REGION The Cordillera Central dominates the midsection of the Dominican Republic. This mountain range starts west of the capital city, Santo Domingo, and rises northwest to the Haitian border. The Cordillera Central contains the highest point in the West Indies—Pico Duarte, at 10,417 feet (3,175 m). In the eastern coastal plain, limestone terraces rise almost 400 feet (122 m) near the foothills of the Cordillera Oriental. In the western edge of the region lies the San Juan Basin.

SOUTHWESTERN REGION Here, the Sierra de Neiba towers over the Hoya de Enriquillo, a bare and dusty valley containing the largest lake in the Caribbean islands. Lake Enriquillo, once part of a strait, is filled with saltwater and lies 150 feet (46 m) below sea level. Crocodiles live in the lake, and flamingos can be found nearby.

The saltwater Lake Enriquillo is named for a Taino hero.

RIVERS

The Yaque del Norte is the longest river in the Dominican Republic, its flow broken only by the Tavera Dam. The river flows through the northern slopes of the Cordillera Central, waters agricultural land in the Cibao Valley, and then forms a delta on the northern coast as it empties into the Atlantic Ocean.

In the south, the Yaque del Sur is the most important river. Flowing through the southern slopes of the Cordillera Central, this river waters the San Juan and Hoya de Enriquillo basins and empties into Neiba Bay on the southern coast, through a delta.

Lake Enriquillo, in the southwest, is the focus of a drainage basin that exceeds 1,158 square miles (3,000 square km) in area, including 102 square miles (265 square km) covered by the salty lake. The basin includes ten minor river systems. The northern rivers flow year-round in the Sierra de Neiba; the southern rivers rise in the Sierra de Bahoruco only after heavy rainfall.

Other rivers include the Yuna, which waters the Vega Real and empties into the Bay of Samaná; the Ozama, which irrigates the Caribbean plain and enters the sea near Santo Domingo; and the Artibonite, which flows west from the Cordillera Central through Haiti to the Golfe de la Gonâve.

Colorful boats are a charming sight in a small fishing harbor at the mouth of the Yuma River.

CLIMATE

Trade winds and high elevations moderate the Dominican Republic's tropical climate. The average annual temperature hovers around 77°F (25°C), with temperatures ranging from 69°F (21°C) in high mountain areas to 82°F (28°C) in coastal areas.

There are two seasons: a rainy season from May to November and a dry season the rest of the year. Moist trade winds from the Atlantic Ocean bring the most rain to the northeast of the country—100 inches (2,540 mm) per year, on average. As they blow across the country, the winds dry out, leaving areas near the Haitian border with little rain—30 inches (760 mm) per year, on average.

Atlantic hurricanes have long pounded Hispaniola. The storms develop during September in the Atlantic Ocean or in the Caribbean Sea. The most destructive hurricanes have killed hundreds of people and caused extensive loss of property. In 1930 a hurricane killed about 8,000 people in

A poinciana tree glows a brilliant red against a blue sky.

the Dominican Republic. In 1998, the Dominican Republic was the hardest hit Caribbean nation in the path of Hurricane George. George produced $1 billion of damage to the Dominican Republic and killed more than 380 people.

FLORA

Due to its diverse geography, the Dominican Republic is home to a variety of plant species. These include the ceiba (silk-cotton) tree, one of the biggest trees in the Central American and Caribbean tropical forest. The indigenous people made practical use of ceiba, crafting canoes from its wood, but the tree also had a spiritual significance for them; it represented the link between heaven and earth.

Plants that these early settlers cultivated are still common in the Dominican Republic today. These include manioc, several kinds of pepper, papaya, tobacco, and the *higuero* (ee-GOOAIR-oh), or calabash tree, which the original inhabitants of Hispaniola used to make ceremonial masks and eating utensils.

The humid mountain forests in the eastern part of the Dominican Republic support lush vegetation. Mahogany trees thrive in abundance; their hard wood was used to build the altar of Santa María la Menor in Santo Domingo, the first cathedral in the Americas.

The higher mountain forests in the Cordillera Central are made up of conifers such as the Creolean pine. Cactus and agave characterize the desert and semiarid areas of the southwest. The coastal flora include mangroves and palms, such as the coconut palm, which was imported from Africa, and the native royal palm. The Spanish settlers introduced food crops such as cocoa, coffee, mangoes, bananas, and sugarcane, and trees such as the African tulip tree and the poinciana, an ornamental tree with bright red, vermillion, orange, and yellow flowers and bright green leaves.

THE CHUPACABRA

A number of people in the Dominican Republic tell of a strange creature that has never been captured or filmed—the chupacabra, or goat sucker. According to eyewitnesses, it has gray skin that is part fur and part feathers. Its short arms end with long nasty claws and its legs are like a kangaroo's legs.

The chupacabra is said to be 4 feet tall when standing erect. Its eyes are huge, elongated, and glowing. The animal is said to be very powerful and people have even reported seeing chupacabras fly.

The creature was first spotted in Puerto Rico in the mid-1990s. A few years later, it was seen in Mexico, South Florida, Central America, and then in the Dominican Republic. Few people have actually seen a chupacabra, but many claim to have seen evidence of the blood-sucking creature in dead cattle and goats with two holes in their neck, with their blood and organs sucked out of them. Some in the Dominican Republic actually believe the creature is an alien brought to Earth in a UFO.

Biologists and wildlife management officials say the creature doesn't really exist, and that it's a myth. They suggest that the creatures thought to be chupacabras might in reality be very sick coyotes that have lost their fur.

FAUNA

One of the most unusual animals in the Dominican Republic is the solenodon, which looks like a rat with an anteater's snout. Solenodons have a poisonous venom similar to some snakes, but the venom has very rarely resulted in human deaths. Another rodent found in the country is the hutia, which looks like a rabbit with short ears and a long tail. Both animals are endangered today.

Other mammals include the West Indian manatee and the bottle-nose dolphin. Humpback whales live in the Bay of Samaná from December through March. The Spanish settlers brought cows, pigs, donkeys, horses, cats, and rats. The mongoose, imported from India to control rats in sugarcane plantations, has multiplied on Hispaniola and has become a pest.

Reptiles, especially snakes, and lizards, are abundant in the country. Tree frogs live on palm trees and even on telephone poles. The American crocodile, rhinoceros iguana, and Ricords iguana are endangered. Scorpions inhabit the drier areas, finding shade under rocks. Spiders are numerous, including tarantulas.

Birds native to the Dominican Republic include mockingbirds, thrashers, woodpeckers, and the rare perico parakeet and Hispaniolan parrot. Fish include grouper, barracuda, parrotfish, leatherjacket, sawfish, Spanish and frigate mackerel, red snapper, mullet, sardines, and eels. The beaches and tidepools yield a variety of crabs and snails.

An old rhinoceros iguana looks as if it has the wisdom of the ages.

CITIES

SANTO DOMINGO The first city founded by Europeans in the Americas, Santo Domingo has many of the region's oldest buildings, such as the first cathedral (Santa María la Menor) and university (Autonomous University of Santo Domingo). Other colonial structures include the Castle of Colón and the Tower of Homage. Restored in the 1970s, the old city preserves its cobblestone streets, outdoor markets, and small craftsmen's shops. Santo Domingo remains the cultural center of the Dominican Republic.

Santo Domingo is the capital, the seat of the national government, and the economic center of the country. The city has a population of more than 3.8 million in the metropolitan area. It attracts the majority of the migrants from the countryside and small towns, and construction rushes to keep up with the influx. Many migrants live in slums in and around the city. Santo Domingo is also home to the suburbs and supermarkets of most of the country's growing middle class.

This view of Santo Domingo suggests a sparkling, modern city.

A monument gleams in a park in Santiago de Los Caballeros.

SANTIAGO DE LOS CABALLEROS With a population of 691,262, Santiago is the Dominican Republic's second-largest city. Besides being the country's agricultural center, Santiago is the capital of Santiago province, and one of the Dominican Republic's cultural, political, industrial, and financial centers. The city and its surrounding countryside is a leading exporter of rum, textiles, and cigars. Santiago is known as "La Ciudad Corazon" (the Heartland City). Santiago is also known as a city of refinement that takes pride in its long tradition of aristocratic families.

LA ROMANA Located on the southern coast, La Romana is a relaxed provincial capital. Traditionally the center of the sugar industry, it is also a popular resort area. La Romana was long considered a company town. In the 1970s the US-based multinational corporation Gulf-Western was one of the largest property owners in the Dominican Republic. The company invested heavily in sugar, cattle, tourism, cement, and real estate. Critics say that the company often employed administrators who bribed local politicians, police officers, and military commanders. To show goodwill, Gulf-Western built schools, churches, clinics, employee housing, recreation centers, and the famous Casa de Campo resort in La Romana. The company sold its holdings in the 1980s.

PUERTO PLATA Located north of Santiago at the foot of Mount Isabel de Torres, Puerto Plata (Silver Port) was founded in 1503 by Christopher Columbus. This scenic city is the center of the Dominican Republic's hotel and resort industry and competes with the capital as the island's top tourist destination. West of Puerto Plata lie the ruins of La Isabela, which Columbus founded in 1493.

Old cannons recall the history of San Felipe Fortress overlooking Puerto Plata Port.

INTERNET LINKS

www.colorado.edu/hazards/publications/sp/sp38/part2.html
This is a report on the damage caused by Hurricane Georges in the Dominican Republic.

www.hispaniola.com/dominican_republic/info/nature_georaphy.php
This is an overview of the Geography of the Dominican Republic

whc.unesco.org/en/list/526
The colonial city of Santo Domingo is a UNESCO World Heritage site.

www.wired.com/2015/03/creature-feature-10-fun-facts-solenodon
This article offers ten fun facts about the amazing solenodon.

HISTORY

A statue in Santo Domingo honors the memory of Christopher Columbus.

DOMINICAN HISTORY IS A STORY of turmoil, war, foreign rule, and *caudillos* (Caw-DEE-ohs)—military dictators who imposed order and stability, often at the cost of freedom. Three times the country has been ruled by foreign nations. Twice it has been ruled by European nations—Spain and France, and twice it has been ruled by nations in the Western Hemisphere—Haiti and the United States. Each time the country has had to struggle for its independence and the right to establish a political system that today, at long last, has established stability without dictatorship as the nation nears the end of the first decade of the twenty-first century.

2

In 1496, Christopher Columbus's brother, Bartholomew Columbus, established the city of Santo Domingo as the capital of the first Spanish colony in the New World.

A rough-hewn canoe in Samana is like those used by the Taino Arawak people five centuries ago.

THE TAINO ARAWAK

When Christopher Columbus (in Spanish, *Cristóbal Colón*) landed on the island of Hispaniola in 1492 and 1493, he met a people who called themselves Taino, a name meaning "good" or "noble," to distinguish themselves from the warlike Carib, who were rumored to be cannibals. Both the Taino and the Carib were members of the Arawak family, the native people of the Greater Antilles and South America. Columbus, of course, called them Indians, thinking that he had reached India in Asia.

Scholars estimate that the population of Hispaniola numbered about 500,000 during the time of the Spanish arrival. Taino Arawak culture had spread throughout much of the Antilles, but the Taino Arawak of Hispaniola and Puerto Rico were the most populous and most culturally complex.

AGRICULTURE The Taino Arawak developed a system of agriculture in which they formed mounds of earth into raised beds called *conuco*

The Taino Arawak believed their ancestors came from caves in a sacred mountain on Hispaniola. Anthropologists say they were descendants of two races originating in Mesoamerica and South America. Hispaniola was originally settled around 4000 BCE by a race of people who moved from Mesoamerica to the islands of Cuba and Hispaniola. These people were supplanted 4,600 years later by descendants of South American Arawak.

The Arawak migrated to the Antilles from the coast of South America sometime in the first millennium bce, supplanting the original inhabitants of the Lesser Antilles, who had also come to the islands from South America, around 2000 BCE. During these centuries of occupation in the Lesser Antilles, Arawak culture changed and adapted. The Arawak finally succeeded in colonizing the eastern tip of Hispaniola around 200 CE.

There they lived for another four hundred years, and their culture continued to evolve. Around 600 CE they spread west across Hispaniola and into the interior. These migrants became the ancestors of the Taino Arawak whom Columbus encountered almost nine hundred years later.

Rock engravings of the Taino culture date to prehistoic times. These are in Isla Cabritos National Park in Lago Enriquillo.

(koh-NOO-koh). On these beds they planted crops such as corn, sweet potatoes, and most importantly manioc, or cassava, a plant that produced a starchy root the Taino Arawak used to make flour for bread. They also cultivated squash, beans, peppers, and peanuts, which were boiled with meat or fish. Around their homes the Taino Arawak planted fruit, calabashes (type of gourd), cotton, and tobacco for cigars. Europeans first learned about tobacco in the Caribbean.

RELIGION The Taino Arawak worshiped deities called *zemis* (SAY-mees), a word that also referred to the idols and fetishes they carried. The supreme deities were Yúcahu, the god of manioc and the sea, and his mother, Atabey, the goddess of fertility and fresh water. Lesser deities included spirits in trees, rocks, and other parts of the landscape, and the spirits of ancestors, who held great importance.

CHIEFS The Taino Arawak lived in homes made from wood and thatch, in villages of 1,000 to 2,000 people. Each village was ruled by a chief called a *cacique* (cah-seek), who could be a man or a woman.

The villages chiefdoms were also organized into district chiefdoms, which were further organized into five regional chiefdoms. The Taino Arawak made sea voyages on trade routes. They traveled in canoes made from ceiba wood; their large canoes could carry up to 150 people.

SPANISH CONQUEST AND COLONIZATION

The promise of gold and silver and other wealth in Hispaniola attracted adventurers from Spain eager to get rich from gold and silver mines on Hispaniola. The Spanish forced the Taino Arawak to work as laborers in the mines and used them mercilessly, forcing them to work long hours, stealing their supplies, and demanding large amounts of tribute from them. Some of the enslaved Indians committed suicide by hanging themselves or drinking poisonous manioc juice to escape Spanish brutality. Many more died from exposure to European diseases, for which they had no immunity. Although peaceful by nature, the Taino Arawak were driven to rebellion in 1495, but the Spaniards crushed the revolt. By 1524 the Taino Arawak had ceased to exist as a people.

In 1503 the colonists of Santo Domingo also began to import slaves from Africa to meet the growing demand for labor in the cultivation of sugarcane. By 1520 the labor force of Santo Domingo consisted almost exclusively of African slaves. The huge tracts of land originally granted by the Spanish crown gave the landowners great power. The political culture of the caudillo,

Bartolomé de Las Casas (1474–1566) was the first priest to be ordained in America, and he was the main advocate for the native peoples of the Americas. He started out as an adventurer and a slave owner, but he soon became appalled by the inhumane treatment of the Indians people and spoke out against the abuse they suffered at the hands of the colonists.

Las Casas spent the rest of his life pressuring the Spanish crown to protect the local people. In 1542 he convinced King Charles V to sign laws abolishing the encomienda system and requiring Spanish colonists to free their slaves. The writings of Las Casas, the first official to decry the injustice of colonial rule, lived on after the man, inspiring independence movements in later centuries.

or military dictator, developed. The caudillos often had magnetic personalities that attracted the loyalty of the people.

By the early sixteenth century, Santo Domingo had begun to decline in riches. The colony stagnated for the next 250 years, as the Spanish crown gave its attention to the richer territories of Mexico and Peru. In the sixteenth and seventeenth centuries, life in Santo Domingo was interrupted only occasionally by armed engagements with French and English pirates. In 1586 the English admiral Sir Francis Drake captured Santo Domingo, demanding a ransom from the Spanish government for its return.

SAINT DOMINGUE AND SANTO DOMINGO

In 1697 Spain signed the Treaty of Ryswick, giving the western third of Hispaniola to France. France named its new colony Saint Domingue, which developed into the most productive colony in the Americas and imported many slaves from Africa to drive its economy.

In 1791 the slaves of Saint Domingue rose up against their owners. A former slave, François-Dominique Toussaint L'Ouverture, formed an army to free the rest of the slaves. Initially, he joined the Spanish forces in their war against France. Later, he joined the French forces against the Spaniards. In 1795 Spain signed the Treaty of Basel, ceding Santo Domingo to France.

Toussaint's goal remained the freedom of his people. He conquered Santo Domingo in 1801 and reformed the government, but in 1802 the French emperor, Napoleon Bonaparte, sent troops to capture L'Ouverture and take him to France. Toussaint died in prison there in 1803. In 1808, Santo Domingo revolted against French rule, and with the help of Great Britain, returned the area to Spanish control.

In 1821 the Dominicans deposed the Spanish governor, José Nuñez de Cáceres, and declared Santo Domingo independent. They called the new nation Spanish Haiti. Before long, the Haitian president, Jean-Pierre Boyer, invaded Spanish Haiti. The Haitian occupation of Santo Domingo from 1821 to 1843 was marked by economic decline and created a deep resentment among the Dominicans toward the Haitians.

INDEPENDENCE

Juan Pablo Duarte, the son of a prominent Santo Domingo family, and a group of supporters called *La Trinitaria*, or "the Trinity," led a revolution against Haitian rule that ended successfully on February 27, 1844, forming the Dominican Republic. The date is now celebrated as Dominican Independence Day, and Duarte, although he never held the office of president, is known as the father of the Dominican Republic.

This engraving, from about 1795, pictures François-Dominique Toussaint L'Ouverture.

TOUSSAINT L'OUVERTURE

Though born a slave in the French colony of Saint Dominique, Toussaint learned of Africa from his father, who had been born a free man in Africa. Toussaint had a liberal master who trained him as a house servant and allowed him to learn to read and write. Toussaint read every book he could get his hands on.

As an adult and an admirer of the French and American revolutions, Toussaint led a slave revolt for freedom. He successfully fought the French as well as invading Spanish and British. By 1803, the French emperor Napoleon agreed to terms of peace with the Haitian revolutionaries. The French commanders invited Toussaint to come to a peace meeting. When he arrived, they arrested him and put him on a ship bound for France, where he died in prison. After his death, Napoleon granted freedom to Haiti. Toussaint's successors conquered and ruled what is now the Dominican Republic from 1821 to 1843, beginning a long-standing dispute between Haiti and the Dominican Republic. Toussaint remains a major historical figure in both Haiti and in the Dominican Republic today.

Unfortunately, Duarte was sick and out of the country when the moment of revolution arrived in 1844. When he returned to the newly named Dominican Republic, the people welcomed him with great adulation and celebration. Within a year of independence, however, a caudillo, or military dictator, Pedro Santana, seized power and exiled Duarte, who spent the rest of his life in Venezuela, where he died in 1876.

Ulises Heureaux

For the next twenty years, two caudillos, General Pedro Santana Familias and General Buenaventura Báez Méndez, fought for power and took turns seizing the presidency. Each used his position to enrich himself, his family, and his supporters at the public's expense.

Santana had the Dominican Republic annexed by Spain in 1861 to protect it from the Haitians. However, the Dominicans rebelled, and in 1865 the Queen of Spain repealed the annexation, prompted in part by the United States. The United States' attention was no longer consumed by the Civil War, and the United States wished to renew its enforcement of the Monroe Doctrine, which prohibited the presence of European powers in the Western Hemisphere.

After Spain's departure, a power struggle ensued between the Dominican Republic's southern region and the northern Cibao region over which region should control the entire country. As a result, the presidency changed hands twelve times between 1865 and 1882.

FROM DICTATORSHIP TO ANARCHY

The power struggles after the restoration in 1865 ended during the presidency of Ulises Heureaux in 1882. In spite of a constitutional two-year term limit, he managed to maintain power until his death in 1899. His personal extravagance and his lavish monetary support of the Dominican secret police resulted in a mounting foreign debt that weighed heavily on the economy. Heureaux was assassinated on July 26, 1899.

The country was plunged into renewed fighting and economic disaster, as foreign governments demanded repayment of the loans Heureaux had incurred. In 1905 the United States increased its interest in Caribbean affairs and signed a financial accord with the Dominican Republic, in which the United States took responsibility for repaying the Dominican Republic's debts by collecting all customs duties and allocating the revenues. This arrangement lasted until 1941.

In 1912, to try to prevent what it saw as a "blackening of the population," the government decreed highly restrictive measures to limit the number of black people allowed to enter the country. The sugar companies ignored the restrictions and brought in Haitian workers in near-slave conditions.

Heated political rivalries continued to create violence and instability. US president Woodrow Wilson sent the US Marines into the Dominican Republic and declared a military government in November 1916. The United States cited fears that Europe would try to intervene in the Dominican conflict, which would be a violation of the Monroe Doctrine.

The Marines restored order throughout most of the country, and economic growth resumed as the military government balanced the budget, reduced the debt, and improved the infrastructure. For the first time, all the regions of the Dominican Republic were linked by roads. The United States also replaced the Dominican military with a professional force called the Dominican Constabulary Guard.

Despite the improvements, Dominicans resented the loss of their independence; nor was the US occupation particularly popular in the United States. On June 21, 1921, US president Warren G. Harding proposed a plan for withdrawal. The final agreement included a few requirements: democratic elections, a loan from the United States of $2.5 million for public works and other expenses, and acceptance of US officers in the National Guard. The US occupation ended with the election of Horacio Vásquez Lajara as president on March 15, 1924. In 1927, however, Vásquez tried to extend his term from four to six years, leading to increased conflicts among rival leaders.

ERA OF TRUJILLO

Dominican factional rivalries were squelched with the election of General Rafael Leonidas Trujillo Molina in 1930. The army ensured his election by harassing and intimidating electoral officials and eliminating potential political opponents. At Trujillo's request, the "Era of Trujillo" was proclaimed by the congress at his inauguration.

Rafael Trujillo, in the dark suit, welcomes the newly-elected Haitian President Paul Magloire, left, in Santo Domingo in February 1951. The army officer in the white uniform behind Trujillo is his brother Hector, who will be the figurehead president from 1952 to 1960.

Trujillo dominated Dominican politics for more than thirty years. He held office from 1930 to 1938, and again from 1942 to 1952, regardless of constitutional term limitations, and in the interim years, he ruled through puppet presidents.

Under Trujillo, the quality of life improved for many Dominicans. The economy expanded, the foreign debt was eliminated, the currency remained stable, the middle class grew, and public-works projects proliferated. Trujillo improved the road system, expanded port facilities, and constructed airports and public buildings. He improved the system of public education, which decreased the illiteracy rate.

There was a dark side to his rule, however. He maintained a secret police force that monitored, and sometimes eliminated, opponents both at home and abroad. He maintained his base of support in the military by paying the officers well, giving them generous side benefits, expanding their forces and equipment, and controlling them through fear. He also used the state to enrich himself enormously; by the end of his rule, the Trujillo family was the largest landowner in the Dominican Republic.

His most outrageous deed was the 1937 massacre of more than 20,000 Haitians living in the Dominican Republic, in retaliation for the Haitian government's execution of his most valued secret agents in Haiti. Trujillo said he was "cleansing" the border region.

Trujillo also became increasingly paranoid about his personal safety. At one point in 1960 he tried to assassinate the Venezuelan president, Rómulo Betancourt, fearing that Betancourt was plotting against him.

The Organization of American States called for an end to diplomatic relations with the Dominican Republic in 1960; the United States broke relations soon after. On May 30, 1961, Trujillo was assassinated with weapons provided by the US Central Intelligence Agency.

WAR AND US INTERVENTION

After a few brief struggles for power, Dominicans elected Juan Bosch Gaviño as president in December 1962 in the country's first free elections in nearly forty years. Bosch was a scholar and poet who, while in exile, had organized opposition to Trujillo through the Dominican Revolutionary Party (PRD). His social and economic policies, such as land reform, demonstrated concern for the welfare of the poor.

Juan Bosch Gaviño

The 1963 constitution separated church and state, guaranteed civil and individual rights, and endorsed civilian control of the military. Powerful institutions such as the military and the church resented these restrictions and warned that the constitution was influenced by Communists and that it would lead to "another Cuba." On September 25, 1963, the military staged a coup.

Bosch supporters and members of the PRD, calling themselves Constitutionalists (in reference to the 1963 constitution), launched a revolution on April 25, 1965. Conservative forces in the military, calling themselves Loyalists, retaliated the next day. The Constitutionalists refused to back down.

On April 28, 1965, the United States sent a force of 20,000 to Santo Domingo in support of the Loyalists, believing that the Constitutionalists were dominated by Communists. A provisional government was established, and elections were organized for July of the following year. Meanwhile, violent skirmishes continued.

Rafael Leonidas Trujillo Molina (1891–1961) was a product of the military constabulary created under the US occupation. He was a commander who came from a humble background. He had enlisted in the National Police in 1918, when upper-class Dominicans were refusing to collaborate with the occupying forces of the United States.

Trujillo rose quickly in the officer corps, all the while building a network of allies and supporters. However much the US officials wanted to see the new military as a professional and apolitical force, Trujillo knew that it was, in fact, the main source of power in the republic, and that it would be his path to power.

He inspired both fear and awe in Dominicans. Because they desired peace and dreaded chaos, the Dominican people admired Trujillo for the order he imposed on society; but they feared the means by which he achieved this order. Many Dominicans remember him today as a stern father.

Rafael Trujillo, on the right, poses for a photograph in 1938.

ECONOMIC REFORMS

The elections of 1966, between the deposed president, Juan Bosch, and Trujillo's designated successor, Joaquín Balaguer, introduced into Dominican politics a rivalry that would continue for decades. Balaguer served as president for twenty-two of the next thirty years. Support for his administration rose and fell with the ups and downs of the republic's sugar-dependent economy.

In 1978 Antonio Guzmán Fernández, the PRD candidate, won the presidency. He combined social and economic reforms with conservative fiscal measures to combat rising oil prices and falling sugar prices. Although his administration suffered from a declining economy and, in 1979, severe hurricane damage, his party retained the presidency in 1982, when Salvador Jorge Blanco was elected president. A recession in the United States and Europe and the Dominican Republic's foreign-debt crisis forced Blanco to implement rationing,

Joaquin Balaguer

which led to riots in 1985. Balaguer won back the presidency in 1986 and was re-elected three times before Leonel Fernández Reyna defeated him in 1996. Balaguer died in 2002.

Leonel Fernández continued Balaguer's work by reducing barriers to trade and encouraging foreign investment through tourism and free-trade zones (FTZs). His first term saw rapid growth in both sectors. In 2000 Hipólito Mejía was elected president. Unfortunately, the economy slowed dramatically after the attacks on the World Trade Center in New York in 2001. High oil prices also limited growth. In 2003 the republic's banks suffered severe crises, and in the elections of 2004, voters rejected Mejía and returned Leonel Fernández to power for a second term.

Large-scale migration from the Dominican Republic to the United States began in the 1960s when the Dominican Republic fell into economic chaos after the 1961 assassination of Rafael Trujillo. The Dominican immigrant population in the United States stood at 12,000 in 1960. By 1990 it was 350,000 and reached 960,000 by 2012. People of Dominican origin or ancestry are now the fifth-largest Hispanic group in the United States, following Mexicans, Puerto Ricans, Cubans, and Salvadorans. Three states—New York, New Jersey, and Florida—are home to 75 percent of Dominican immigrants. Many send back money to relatives in the Dominican Republic. In 2012, Dominicans in the United States sent back $3.6 billion, representing 6 percent of the country's gross domestic product (GDP).

Fernández was re-elected in 2008 and is credited with pushing the country forward in terms of technology, including the construction of the Metro Railway ("El Metro),the largest subway and rail system in the Caribbean and Central American region. El Metro is part of a major "National Master Plan" to improve transportation throughout the Dominican Republic.

Danilo Medina, elected president in 2012, has continued to upgrade the technology infrastructure in the Dominican Republic and, in addition, he has spent more money to improve schools throughout the nation. International criticism of his treatment of Dominicans of Haitian descent, however, has complicated his term in office.

Dominican President Leonel Fernandez conducts the train of a new subway line in Santo Domingo on February 27, 2012.

INTERNET LINKS

www.donquijote.org/culture/dominican-republic/society/people/juan-pablo-duarte
This is a quick biography of Juan Pablo Duarte, the "father of the Dominican Republic."

latinamericanhistory.about.com/od/historyofthecaribbean/p/The-Us-Occupation-Of-The-Dominican-Republic-1916-1924.htm
The story of the US occupation of the Dominican Republic from 1916 to 1924

www.mapsofworld.com/flags/dominican-republic-flag.html
This explains the story of the Dominican flag.

GOVERNMENT

The flag of the Dominican Republic flies at the National Palace in Santo Domingo.

3

The Dominican Republic is the only country in the world with a picture of a Bible on its flag.

ON PAPER, THE DOMINICAN REPUBLIC is a democracy where every adult is allowed to vote. But, at least in the past, reality has been different. Too often the government has been run by a strong caudillo for the benefit of himself and well-connected friends and allies. In much of Dominican history, even though the government structure has been modelled after a democracy, informal connections— "whom you know"—have been where the real levers of power are pulled. Since the end of the Trujillo dictatorship, the Dominican Republic has become more of a real democracy, but most outside observers will say the country still has many of the earmarks of a country run by a small group of well-connected people.

VOTING

Voting is compulsory in the Dominican Republic for all citizens eighteen years or older and for any married individuals regardless of age. The requirement is not enforced, however. Members of the police or armed forces are not allowed to vote, as well as prisoners. Ballots are color-coded to compensate for the high rate of illiteracy. Voters receive two separate ballots for each of the competing political parties. They deposit one for the presidential election and one for all other contested offices. This system, in effect, forces the voter to elect a party rather than an individual to office, thus explaining why the president's party almost always carries a majority in congress.

THE PRESIDENCY

The president and the vice-president of the Dominican Republic are directly elected. They are limited to a four-year term but may run for re-election. The president appoints a cabinet of around twenty department heads and,

A man casts his ballot at a polling station in Santo Domingo on election day in 2012.

Emerging from the Trujillo era, Dominicans desired a firm commitment to constitutionalism, that is, loyalty to a set of governing principles rather than loyalty to a leader. The constitutionalist ideal was not popular with aspiring caudillo, but the constitution first adopted on November 28, 1966 has lasted to the present, with major reforms enacted in 2010.

The 2010 document forms a compromise between the authoritarian history of the Dominican Republic and the ideals of democracy. While it establishes a lengthy list of basic rights and civil liberties and provided for a strengthened legislature, it also grants a great deal of power to the president, including emergency measures that, whenever exercised, historically have preceded a slide into dictatorship.

The 2010 constitution also reaffirms and strengthens several basic democratic principles that traditionally had been present in the Dominican Republic, but not always exercised. These basic principles included representative government by direct vote; the separation of powers into executive, legislative, and judicial branches; a system of checks and balances between the branches of government; and the right to civil and political liberties.

The Dominican constitution defines few limitations on the president's power. It requires him to obtain congressional consent for certain appointments, treaty negotiations, and entry into certain contracts, and for the use of emergency powers. With the Dominican electoral system, however, the president's party almost always holds a majority in congress, so his wishes are rarely at risk of being defeated.

as executive, has authority over the appointment and dismissal of almost all public officials.

The Dominican Republic has a strong executive office. The constitution gives the president the power to promulgate laws passed by congress; to engage in diplomatic relations; and to command, deploy, and make appointments in the armed forces. His extensive emergency powers include the authority to suspend basic civil rights in times of emergency, to postpone congressional sessions, to declare a state of siege, and to rule by decree.

THE LEGISLATURE

The 2010 constitution gives all legislative powers to the bicameral National Congress, which consists of the Senate and the Chamber of Deputies. Members

Danilo Medina Sanchez was born in 1951 in the Dominican Republic. He is the oldest of eight brothers. Even as a high school student he was interested in politics and government. At age eighteen he founded the San Juan de la Maguana branch of a national political party. When professor Juan Bosch founded the Partido de la Liberacion Dominicana in 1973 (PLD), Medina joined him. He studied economics at the Instituto Tecnological Santo Domingo (INTEC) and graduated magna cum laude in 1984. In 1987 he was elected a deputy in the Dominican Congress.

Medina was elected President of the Dominican Republic in the 2012 with 51.24 percent of the vote. Since taking office he has vowed to fight corruption, create jobs, and, most importantly, invest in improving education in the Dominican Republic. He has also come under international criticism for his government's treatment of people of Haitian descent in the Dominican Republic. Medina can run for re-election in 2016 for another four-year term.

of both houses are directly elected for four-year terms, which are staggered across presidential terms.

The Senate has thirty-two seats, and the Chamber of Deputies has 150 seats. Each of the country's thirty-one provinces elects a senator, as does the National District. Deputies are elected by proportional representation from the provinces. A province with a large population will be represented by more deputies than one with a smaller population.

The constitution gives the congress the power to control immigration, change internal administrative boundaries, declare a state of emergency, legislate on matters of public debt and matters outside executive and judicial authority, examine presidential initiatives, levy taxes, and question cabinet ministers (although it does not confirm them for office), among others.

The legislative branch had a negligible role under the strong arm of the caudillo. Even with its constitutional powers after 1966, it remained weak during the Balaguer years. Only in 1978, with democracy fully restored under presidents Guzmán Fernández and Jorge Blanco, was the National Congress finally able to start acting on its constitutional powers. Though not yet fully independent of the president's control, it is developing as an important balance to the nation's strong executive office.

Members of Congress gather for the official swearing in of President Danilo Medina.

THE JUDICIARY

The judicial branch of government is headed by a supreme court, which consists of sixteen members. It is the ultimate court of appeal and tries any case involving the president, vice-president, designated cabinet members, and members of congress. The Supreme Court also administers the entire judicial system which includes courts of first instance and courts of appeal, and can dismiss or transfer lower-court judges.

Judges serve four-year renewable terms coinciding with the presidential term. Supreme-court justices are appointed by the National Judicial Council, consisting of the president of the Dominican Republic, leaders of both houses of the congress, the president of the supreme court, and an opposition-party member. The council was created after the 1994 elections, to curb the power of the president to appoint the highest judges in the land without consultation. The judiciary remains the weakest branch of government.

A NONPOLITICAL MILITARY

The Dominican government recognizes the importance of a professional, nonpolitical military, but the armed forces continue to influence domestic politics, although more indirectly than before. The government has, since 1978, actively worked to reduce the political role of the armed forces. Members of the armed forces and the police are not allowed to vote or to participate in

Members of the Dominican Armed Forces march in a military parade on February 27, 2015, in Santo Domingo to celebrate the country's 171 years of independence.

the activities of political parties or labor unions. The armed forces consist of the army, the navy, and the air force. The combined strength of these forces totals 44,000, equalling five military personnel for every thousand citizens. The military is involved in stopping drug trafficking and patrolling the Haitian border for illegal immigrants.

Although the Dominican Republic has not confronted any serious external threats for years, it still perceives Haiti and Cuba as potential threats to national security. Haiti is a concern due to internal political upheavals that could spill over the border in the form of refugees. The Dominican Republic does not fear an overt attack by Cuba but that Cuba could support Dominican dissidents, inspiring them to revolt, as happened in 1959 during the Trujillo dictatorship.

The armed forces' unofficial mission is to maintain internal security and public order. Only a few underground insurgency groups remain in operation in the Dominican Republic, however, and they represent little threat to internal security.

While the national police are officially responsible for maintaining internal security, they are often aided by the armed forces. The armed forces have been summoned in the recent past to assist the police in quelling civil unrest in the form of strikes and protest rioting, especially during the 1980s and again in 2003 and 2004.

INTERNET LINKS

www.miamiherald.com/news/nation-world/world/americas/article1952530.html
The Dominican army fights crime in Santo Domingo.

unpan1.un.org/intradoc/groups/public/documents/un-dpadm/unpan048943.pdf
This is the full text of the Dominican Constitution.

ECONOMY

A vivid sunrise announces a beautiful day on a sandy beach in the Dominican Republic.

4

THE DOMINICAN REPUBLIC HAS THE largest economy in the Caribbean region. Its 2014 per capita GDP (total value of goods and services divided by population) was US $13,000. The main economic growth in the last decade for the Dominican Republic have been tourism and light manufacturing. Many Dominicans have made fortunes in both these sectors. Despite such growth, the Dominican Republic remains a relatively poor nation by world standards. Income distribution remains wildly divided between a small number of rich people and a huge majority of very poor people. Although President Medina and his government have pledged to narrow the gap between rich and poor, centuries of economic and educational inequality have made the effort difficult.

Organic farming is a small but growing agricultural industry in the Dominican Republic. Organic crops fill a niche market that is aimed at wealthy customers, particularly in the European Union. Today, the major organic exports in the Dominican Republic are bananas, cocoa, coffee, and mangos.

FARMING

Previously, agriculture was the economic foundation and the main employer in the Dominican Republic; in 2014 it accounted for only 6.3 percent of the country's gross domestic product (GDP) and employed only 14.4 percent of the Dominican workforce.

Historically, tight import restrictions forced the Dominicans to grow most of their own food and rely on sugar exports for the bulk of their foreign earnings. Today Dominicans import food and export many cash crops such as coffee, cocoa, and tobacco. This shift was made to increase foreign currency earnings in order to meet the requirements of international financial institutions.

Latifundios (lah-tee-FOON-dyos), or large landholdings, account for only 2 percent of Dominican farms, but they control 55 percent of the farmland. In contrast, *minifundios* (mee-nee-FOON-dyos), which are landholdings smaller than 50 acres (20 hectares), account for 82 percent of Dominican farms but occupy only 12 percent of the farmland. Tens of thousands of campesinos own no more than a few *tareas* (tah-RAY-as), a unit equivalent to 0.15 acres (0.06 hectares).

SUGAR The Dominican Republic is the tenth-largest sugar producer in the world. Sugar is its largest agricultural export. The world price of sugar and the success of the harvest have a dramatic impact on Dominicans. Tens of thousands of Dominicans in the fields, mills, refineries, distilleries, and shipyards

Beans ripen on the branches of a coffee plant.

depend on sugar for a living. Sugar prices have generally declined since 1980. Higher oil prices, global economic recessions, and greater competition among producers have pushed sugar prices down. Beet sugar produced in temperate areas, such as the United States and Europe, has reduced demand for tropical cane sugar. Hurricane Georges in 1998 devastated the main sugar-producing region around La Romana and Boca Chica.

Many of the large sugar plantations are owned by private investors. There are also independent cane growers called *colonos* (koh-LOH-nohs), who sell directly to the mills. As their small landholdings become fragmented, fewer growers can survive from sugar.

COFFEE Most coffee farms in the Dominican Republic are small land-holdings run by farmers who make their living growing coffee. Coffee production fell drastically following Hurricane Georges. In addition to rebuilding their farms and livelihood, small-scale coffee growers have been working to improve their farming methods with the government's assistance. Governmental initiatives were implemented to improve the quality of Dominican coffee and promote its reputation and competitiveness in world markets.

Leaves of tobacco dry on a rope under the roof of a cigar factory.

TOBACCO First cultivated by the Taino Arawak, tobacco enjoyed a renaissance in the Dominican Republic during the 1960s with the introduction of new varieties and an increased market price. It peaked as an export crop in 1978, then declined in the 1980s due to disease, deteriorating prices, and inadequate marketing. Black tobacco is the variety that is manufactured into cigars for export. It accounted for over 80 percent of the harvest in 2014.

The Dominican Republic is the world's largest cigar exporter. It produced more than 1.7 billion cigars in the 2012—2013 cigar harvest. In that same time period, cigar exports generated $577.3 million for the country and the cigar industry was responsible for around 108,935 jobs. More and more foreign cigar companies operate out of the Dominican Republic, taking advantage of its free-trade zones (FTZs). The earnings of these companies do not contribute directly to national accounts, but the local revenue and the jobs they offer contribute to the country's economic overall growth.

NONTRADITIONAL CROPS Falling prices for traditional crops in the 1980s persuaded the Dominican government to promote nontraditional crop exports. Successful nontraditional crops include ornamental plants, winter vegetables (vegetables not grown in the United States in winter), citrus and tropical fruit, spices, nuts, and the distinctive produce popular with the Hispanic population in the United States. The conversion to nontraditional crops was aided by the Caribbean Basin Initiative, which provided duty-free access to the US market for some 3,000 products.

FOOD CROPS Rice, the main ingredient in the national dish, was the Dominican Republic's most important food crop. Rice production in the country has fallen since 1979 and can no longer meet domestic demand, forcing the country to import rice.

Other major food crops include corn (which is native to the island), sorghum, plantains, beans, and assorted tubers. Dominican farmers also grow various kinds of fruit, vegetables, spices, and nuts, including bananas, guavas, tamarinds, passionfruit, coconuts, tomatoes, carrots, lettuce, cabbages, scallions, onions, garlic, coriander, and peanuts.

A field of rice in the Dominican Republic reflects the dramatic sky.

LIVESTOCK The Dominican Republic raises enough livestock for domestic use as well as export. Livestock ranches consist primarily of beef and dairy cattle, poultry, and swine. Cattle ranching, the basis of the economy in the mid-nineteenth century, remains important. The main export commodities are hides and salted beef.

FORESTRY

The government prohibited commercial tree cutting in 1967 to counter the effects of slash-and-burn agriculture and indiscriminate tree cutting. The remaining forests, covering 22 percent of the land, consist mainly of pine and hardwood.

Plantation forestry provides timber products for domestic use, but wood products are still imported to meet demand. The government is working toward replacing some of the lost forest.

MINING

The Dominican Republic's most important minerals include ferronickel, bauxite, and a gold-silver alloy called Dore. Lesser minerals include iron, limestone, copper, gypsum, mercury, salt, sulfur, marble, onyx, and travertine. Marble, onyx, and travertine are industrial minerals.

The government fueled a rapid growth in the mining sector during the 1970s when it invited foreign companies to search for minerals. The second largest ferronickel mine in the world is the Falcondo Mine in Bonao, northwest of Santo Domingo, and ferronickel is the country's biggest mineral export.

This is a specimen of falcondoite, a rare, nickel-rich mineral from the Dominican Republic.

MANUFACTURING

Manufacturing accounted for about 32 percent of the GDP and employed almost 21 percent of the Dominican Republic's workforce in 2014. Food and beverage processing made up more than half of Dominican manufacturing activities. Manufacturing firms also produced chemicals, textiles, and nonmetallic minerals.

Along with many developing countries, the Dominican Republic has opened its doors to free trade zones (FTZs), areas that are given special status so that businesses producing goods within them are not subject to taxes. FTZs in the Dominican Republic tend to be built near ports. Foreign businesses import parts, assemble products in the FTZs, and export the products to their destination markets.

FTZ expansion in the Dominican Republic has been phenomenal, bringing foreign investment and innovation, but jobs in FTZs usually pay poorly. While many Dominican women benefit from holding non-traditional jobs in FTZs, tension may develop in some homes where the woman earns more than her underemployed husband.

Dominican women work at machines at a typical clothing factory.

The main FTZ industries in the Dominican Republic are clothing, electronics, footwear, jewellery, furniture, perfume, and pharmaceuticals. FTZs also contain call centers and data-entry enterprises, which have bolstered jobs in the service sector. One of the newest FTZs being developed is the Cyber Park near Santo Domingo. It will house computer firms, a golf course, and a training school for workers.

CONSTRUCTION

Construction activity showed remarkable growth in the Dominican Republic in 2014. The Dominican government encouraged the building of highways,

schools, and hotels, spurring a growth in jobs not seen since the 1990s. According to information provided by the Dominican Republic Central Bank, the construction sector of the nation's economy showed a 2014 growth rate of 13.8 percent, almost twice the national economic growth rate of just over 7 percent.

Such projects as the Duarte Corridor (a major road infrastructure project), the second line of the Santo Domingo Metro, and the construction of 10,000 new classrooms, as well as new hotel construction spurred the construction industry.

Construction workers build concrete forms for the metro system in Santo Domingo.

ENERGY

With no oil or coal of its own, the Dominican Republic struggles with an energy problem. Some of its rivers produce hydroelectric power but not enough for the demands of a growing population and economy. High-energy prices and rolling blackouts are common.

TOURISM

Dominican Republic airports recorded a record 5,141,377 tourists visiting the nation in 2014. The figure is an almost 9 percent increase over 2013. In December 2014, the Dominican Republic welcomed two new world class resorts on the nation's north coast that the Dominican Republic expects record tourism to only increase from 2015 onward.

While tourism creates jobs, it strains the infrastructure and is unpredictable and vulnerable to global economic ups and downs. To help with the increase in tourists, in 2014 the government constructed a new highway connecting Santo Domingo with Punta Cana that sliced the driving time from four hours to two hours.

BOOM OR BUST

The Dominican Republic has experienced some of the most dramatic growth rates in the Caribbean as a result of expanded tourism and FTZ investment. Those well placed to take advantage of these booms have become wealthy, but neither sector has produced stable, permanent, well-paid jobs in significant numbers, so most Dominicans have not benefited much.

Laundry dries outside at a Haitian refugee camp on a sugar cane plantation in the Dominican Republic.

By 2015, the country was still plagued by serious inequalities, with the richest 10 percent of the population earning 40 percent of the wealth and the poorest 50 percent of the population earning less than 20 percent of the wealth. The nation has to find a balance between economic growth and stability so that poor Dominicans can get a chance at a better life.

INTERNET LINKS

assets.coca-colacompany.com/e5/1a/ cd3d5c2b49ab93599bbb8200716d/DominicanSugarIndustry-AMacroLevelReport.pdf
Here you can find a history of sugar in the Dominican Republic from the Coca-Cola Company.

cotni.org/news/dominican-republic/2007/11/14/origin-dominican-batey
This is a history of sugar in the Dominican Republic from another point of view.

www.planetware.com/tourist-attractions/dominican-republic-dom.htm
This travel site lists the top tourist attractions in the Dominican Republic.

ENVIRONMENT

A young humpback whale breaches in the Caribbean Sea.

5

THE DOMINICAN REPUBLIC FACES the same environmental challenges that all nations in the twenty-first century face. With economic growth and rapid population growth, protecting both land and water have become a priority for Dominicans. The problem becomes even more urgent to solve because the island nation depends on clean oceans, land, and beaches to attract tourists. You can't advertise yourself as a tropical paradise if oil and waste and manufacturing runoff are major environmental problems. Fortunately, the Dominican Republic is well aware of this and working to fight pollution.

THE IMPORTANCE OF WATER

The Dominican Republic is surrounded by water, but water is a scarce resource on the island. Saltwater sustains only certain forms of life; land plants and animals, including humans, require fresh water to survive.

The famous El Limon waterfall makes a thrilling sight in the Dominican rainforest.

Dominicans get the fresh water they need from rain. Most rain falls on the highlands, where rivers carry the water into the lowlands and out to sea. Most rain is caused by ocean and air currents, but research suggests that tropical forests can contribute to the conditions necessary for rainfall through the release of water from the leaves of trees and by creating updrafts of cooler air. Also, the roots of trees anchor the soil so that it acts like a sponge, absorbing rainwater that would otherwise wash the soil away.

Human activity easily upsets this delicate natural system. Forests are cleared to make way for farms to grow crops to feed the growing population, and, without alternative sources of energy, wood is used as fuel for cooking. If there are no tree roots to absorb rainwater, raging rivers form that can cause floods and destroy human settlements; soil is washed out to sea, where it can choke coral reefs and kill fish.

Dominican waterways need protection from pollution. Pesticides used on plantations get washed by rain into rivers, which become more contaminated when urban sewage is dumped into them. This flows out to sea, where it destroys marine life and makes swimming hazardous.

Without vibrant coral reefs and clean beaches to draw tourists to the coastal resorts, urban dwellers have fewer jobs. If safeguards are not implemented to protect waterways, Dominicans risk destroying the ecosystems that sustain life. Their challenge in the immediate future is to balance competing uses of fresh water with everyone's dependence on it to make their living.

FIRST STEPS IN ENVIRONMENTAL PROTECTION

From the time of Columbus to the 1960s, about 77 percent of the Dominican Republic's original forest cover was cleared to make way for plantations and then the lumber industry. In the 1960s the government banned commercial logging and started forest reserves and parks. This dramatically slowed, but did not stop, deforestation. People in rural areas still needed wood for fuel and land to farm.

In 2000, for the first time in decades, the government addressed environmental policy and passed the Environmental Framework Law. The law created the first Dominican Ministry of the Environment and Natural Resources, which is charged with regulating the use of natural resources such as water and forests. Its mandate is to seek cooperation from private business interests and communities in creating sustainable practices that balance competing human needs with the requirements of preservation. There are signs that Dominicans will find a way to live within the limits set by nature. For example, the Sabana Yegua Model Forest, set up in 2003, offers a novel approach to forest management. Rather than stay out of the forest altogether, the local people learn to cut trees selectively and to plant consistently so that there is always a supply of trees for wood and fuel.

Young banana trees grow on a plantation in the rainforest.

People are also encouraged to plant fruit and nut trees so that they benefit from the living forest rather than earning a living by the death of the forest. Learning how to use the forest instead of seeing it as an obstruction to farming and other activities encourages people to get involved in forest maintenance. Protecting the forest guarantees less soil erosion and more fresh water for all Dominicans. It has the added advantage of reducing the risk of flooding and damage to coral reefs. Such an integrated approach benefits everyone.

From January through March each year, some three thousand to five thousand humpback whales migrate to Bahía de Samaná (Samaná Bay) on the northeastern coast of the Dominican Republic.

Humpbacks are a delight to watch because they are very active and visible. They sometimes breach, or throw their entire body out of the water, and they can swim upside down with their fins out of the water. Also, they communicate by raising their huge tails out of the water and slapping them down. Many people have heard their famous "songs," patterned sequences of noises that males sometimes emit while hanging their head down in deep water. Scientists do not know what the songs are for, but all whales in the same population, such as those in the North Atlantic, sing the same song, which is distinct from the songs sung by other populations, such as those in the North Pacific.

Humpbacks spend part of the year in the frigid waters of the Arctic, where they feed on small organisms that they strain through the baleen in their mouths. They migrate to warmer and shallower waters, such as those around Hispaniola and Samaná, so that fertile females can mate and give birth. During this period, whales fast, since there is no food in the water for them. A humpback calf weighs about a ton at birth and will stay with its mother for the first year of life. She will protect it and nurse it with her rich milk. While mother and calf are in warm water, the mother does not eat, while the calf can consume up to one hundred gallons of her milk a day. All adult whales lose about 25 percent of their body weight during their tropical water visits, while calves gain up to one hundred pounds every day in preparation for their first trip into colder waters.

FUTURE OF ENVIRONMENTAL PROTECTION

The Dominican Republic is a small country with big environmental challenges. The government is implementing projects that meet the needs of all parties and encourage conservation as part of long-term economic management.

In the end, Dominicans will benefit from cleaner water, healthier forests, and the money visitors spend to enjoy this island paradise. The Dominican Republic now receives more than 5 million tourists every year. One of the fastest-growing sectors of the economy, tourism provides a strong incentive for environmental protection, because so much is at stake.

One of the Dominican Republic's protected natural attractions are the whales in the Bay of Samaná. Every year from January to March 10,000 North Atlantic humpback whales come to the warmer waters of the Caribbean to perform their intricate mating dance and give birth to the next generation. Whales must surface every 15 to 45 minutes to breathe. Humpbacks, being fairly slow-moving, especially in shallow waters, have been easy targets for whalers. In 1966 they became protected by the International Whaling Commission. Today it is estimated that there are about 35,000 to 40,000 humpbacks worldwide, or about 35 percent of their peak population.

INTERNET LINKS

www.accessdr.com/2012/10/samana-worlds-most-important-sanctuary-for-humpback-whales
Here you can find pictures, a map, and a short article about the humpback whales in Samaná Bay.

imfn.net/sabana-yegua-model-forest
An overview of the Sabana-Yegua Model Forest

www.sustainabletrip.org/blog/index.cfm/2013/4/2/Tourists-Help-Restore-Coral-Reefs-in-the-Dominican-Republic
An article explains how tourists are helping restore coral reefs in the Dominican Republic.

DOMINICANS

A Dominican worker at a luxury oceanfront condo development poses for a picture.

6

THE PEOPLE OF THE DOMINICAN Republic truly form a "melting pot" of races: black, Indian, and European. Light-skinned Dominicans identify themselves as white; those of mixed ancestry call themselves Indian; and Dominicans of Haitian ancestry are black. Generally, upper-class Dominicans tend to have lighter skin than Dominicans in the lower classes.

Today there are more Dominicans living in New York City than in Santiago, the second-most populated city of the Dominican Republic.

RACE AND CLASS

Although the Dominican Republic was Spain's oldest colony in the Americas, it has the shallowest family ancestral roots. Spaniards came to the island seeking gold or land, but they often moved on to mainland America for economic or political reasons. Thus, for many white Dominicans, their ancestry on Hispaniola spans no more than six generations. Historically, the black population was anchored by slavery and servitude, but these same institutions made it difficult to trace the roots of black Dominicans. More recently, Dominicans of all skin colors and classes have migrated from the island's rural areas to its cities and beyond, to Puerto Rico and mainland America.

Only 16 percent of the Dominican population is white or of pure European ancestry. The proportion of blacks is even lower—only

11 percent. About 73 percent of the population is of mixed ancestry. Immigrants make up a tiny proportion of the island's population, but they come from near and far: Haiti, the West Indies, the United States, Lebanon, Italy, France, China, and Japan.

Although more than two-thirds of Dominican society is mulatto, of mixed black and white ancestry, most Dominicans deny their African ancestry and ignore African influences on their culture. In the 1880s, some intellectuals advocated a celebration of mulatto culture, but such racial pride was swept away during Trujillo's rule.

A mulatto himself, Trujillo rewrote Dominican history and racial identities to deny African elements in the population and culture. He created a national ideology of *hispanidad* (ees-pah-nee-DAHD), which defined Dominicans as the most Spanish people of America.

A military woman holds the flag in a parade in Santo Domingo in 2014.

Today Dominicans identify themselves as either white or Indian. Official identification cards do not mention mulattos, and the term black is reserved for Haitians. Dominicans like to describe their skin color as *café con leche*, or coffee with milk, but they attribute this to their Indian background.

The military is one of few avenues for upward social and economic mobility for poor Dominicans. In fact, the Dominican Republic has had more black and mulatto presidents than any other Western Hispanic nation.

A small, elite group commands a great proportion of Dominican wealth and power, while the majority of the population lives in poverty. Socially, the primary division is between the gentility—called *la gente buena* (la HEN-tay BUAY-nah), literally good people, or *la gente culta* (la HEN-tay KOOL-tah), literally refined people—and the common masses. While the masses struggle from day to day, *la gente buena* adhere to traditional Hispanic ideals of dignity, leisure, grandeur, and generosity.

UPPER CLASS

The Dominican Republic did not develop a true landowning class until the late 1800s, almost two hundred years later than most Latin American countries. The primary source of social identity for the mostly white oligarchy is through kinship ties, which also provide the pool from which business partners and political allies are selected.

In Santo Domingo and Santiago, the upper class is divided into two sections: *la gente de primera* (la HEN-tay day pree-MAY-rah), or first people; and *la gente de segunda* (la HEN-tay day say-GOON-dah), or second people. *La gente de primera* include a hundred families that constitute the cream of the upper class. They are locally referred to as the *tutumpote* (too-toom-POH-tay), or totem pole, implying family worship and excessive concern with ancestry. *La gente de segunda* include descendants of the business elite that emerged in the early twentieth century, and the *nuevos ricos* (NUAY-vohs REE-kohs), or new rich, who emerged with the rise of Trujillo. The newest elites have acquired their wealth through banking, professional occupations, light industry, and tourism.

The upper class concerns itself with national and international issues, such as world sugar prices, US power and investments, trade patterns, the future of tourism, the need for social and political order and improved infrastructure, and the complex web of family ties and associated gossip.

A lab technician studies disease-carrying mosquitoes in a public health lab in Santo Domingo.

MIDDLE CLASS

The expansion of the sugar industry in the late nineteenth century broadened the ranks of the middle class to include professionals, small shopkeepers, teachers, and clerical employees. Today, the middle class constitutes 30 to 35 percent of the population and is concentrated among the salaried professionals in the government and private sectors.

The middle class lacks a sense of class identity partly due to the fact that its members rely on the patron-client system to move ahead rather than on any common bond of social or economic interest. Moreover, those with dark skin or limited finances have limited opportunities for social mobility. The upper-middle class is mostly white, but most middle-class Dominicans are mulattos.

The members of the middle class like to consider themselves part of *la gente buena*, at least in spirit. To the extent that they are able, they adopt the attitudes and lifestyle espoused by the elites. However, they have no independent sources of wealth and are vulnerable to the economic cycles of the country. This reinforces the patron-client system, since they must rely on patronage rather than political action when ill winds blow.

The concerns of the middle class center on expanding their wealth and extending their network of social and political influence. As they rise, they are in turn expected to reward their family and friends.

LOWER CLASS

The concerns of two-thirds of Dominicans center on issues of daily survival. Mostly illiterate and unskilled, they struggle for food, shelter, and clothing, because there are not enough jobs to go around. A quarter of them are unemployed.

RURAL POOR Two types of campesinos characterize the countryside: subsistence farmers and landless wage workers. For every small land-holder, there are ten to twenty wage workers competing for whatever jobs are available. Most small rural neighborhoods in the country are very close-knit. They were originally settled by one or two families whose descendants developed extensive kinship ties through intermarriage and *compadrazgo* (kom-pah-DRAHZ-goh), or "god parentage." Campesinos usually live close to a water source in small groups of houses connected by narrow dirt paths. They depend on their neighbors and kin for assistance and tend to distrust outsiders.

Among the Dominican rural poor, almost all women contribute to the family income, and they are increasingly left to run the household alone as the men leave to seek work. The women earn money by cultivating garden plots, raising livestock for sale, and selling various items from lottery tickets to homemade sweets. They also work during the labor-intensive phases of harvesting cotton, coffee, and tobacco, but they earn less than their male counterparts and are paid by the unit rather than on a daily basis.

A young woman carries sacks of dried tobacco in a cigar factory.

URBAN POOR In 1920, 80 percent of Dominicans lived in rural areas. By 2015, it was the reverse: 79 percent live in rapidly expanding urban areas.

Campunos (kahm-POO-nohs), or "rural-to-urban migrants", are seeking employment, but they find instead overcrowded slums with malnourished children, no electricity, no running water, and no sewage facilities. National unemployment in 2014 was 6.4 percent, and more than 20 percent of the population lives in poverty. The rate of underemployment is even higher; many have jobs but cannot earn enough for their needs. A large proportion of urban households are headed by women who often earn money more consistently than men.

Small neighborhoods are the center of social life for the urban poor. As in the rest of Dominican society, the urban poor turn to neighbors and kin for

The Dominican Day Parade in New York City is an annual event held in August on Sixth Avenue to show the pride of the large Dominican population. It started in 1982 as a small celebration with concerts and cultural events. Today, it has become a large event, with Dominicans dressing up in national costumes and Dominican bands playing traditional music.

Smaller Dominican Day parades are also held in August in Paterson, NJ, Boston, and along the Grand Concourse in the Bronx. The New York City parade is put on by the Dominican Day Parade, Inc., a group that includes many distinguished Dominican immigrants in all areas of civic life.

assistance in times of need. Migrants maintain ties with their family back in the countryside through a *cadena* (kah-DAY-nah), or "chain," of mutual assistance. People in the countryside take care of the family or land of those who leave, while people in the city help new *campunos* find work and a place to stay.

HAITIANS

There are over 500,000 Haitians and Dominicans of Haitian descent living in the Dominican Republic. Most came as agricultural workers to cut sugarcane or harvest coffee, rice, or tomatoes. Some came to escape the grinding poverty of Haiti, while others were recruited by Dominican agents known as *buscones* (boos-KOHN-ays). Haiti has been a source of cheap labor for the Dominican Republic for decades, until, in 1986, a formal agreement between the two countries permitted a fixed number of Haitians to cross the border to work.

With the privatization of government industries, the already miserable conditions of Haitian cane cutters got worse. They live in *bateyes* (bah-TAY-ays), settlements around the fields in Barahona, Puerto Plata, and Santo Domingo, in tiny shacks with no sanitation. They work thirteen hours a day for very little pay, and children sometimes work alongside adults. They have no security; the government may repatriate them anytime to appease racism and xenophobia among Dominicans. With the economic downturn in the twenty-first century, Haitians, Dominicans of Haitian descent, and blacks in general have been blamed for lowering wages and taking jobs. They are regularly rounded up in the thousands by the military and trucked across the border. International human rights organizations are involved in defending these people's legal rights.

A typical batey on a sugar cane plantation shows the impoverished living conditions.

INTERNET LINKS

www.biography.com/people/groups/dominican
Here is a compilation of some famous Dominicans and Dominican-Americans.

www.huffingtonpost.com/jamele-rigolini/four-facts-about-poverty-_b_6820048.html
This is a quick but insightful overview of poverty in Latin America.

www.makariosinternational.org/life-in-a-batey.html
"Life in a Batey" offers a look at rural poverty in the Dominican Republic.

www.theroot.com/articles/history/2011/08/dominicans_and_race_dont_call_them_black.html
"Dominicans in Denial" is an excellent article about race in the Dominican Republic.

LIFESTYLE

Women agricultural employees work in a field in Polo.

7

THE DOMINICAN LIFESTYLE IS often characterized as a cheerful acceptance of life with both its joys and sorrows and willingness to share everything with family and friends. Dominican families are often large, with many brothers, sisters, cousins, etc., all sharing life together and enjoying the year's celebrations.

Teen pregnancy is common in the Dominican Republic. In 2013, one in ten teen girls became pregnant. Health workers are trying to educate young people to reverse this trend.

A family enjoys a midday rest in a village near Barahona.

Because family and friends are so important in Dominican culture, many decisions, both public and private comes from a network of personal relationships. Dominicans of all classes greatly depend on kinship ties for land, employment, childcare, economic assistance, and political positions.

BIRTH

A particular set of customs and beliefs, affecting both mother and child, accompany the birth process, especially in rural areas and among the lower classes. For example, in many areas, the mother must avoid eating fruit

A mother holds her baby in a very poor section of San Pedro de Macoris.

(especially bananas) when pregnant lest the baby be born with phlegm in the chest. She must also abstain from eating charred or crusty food that gets stuck to the cooking kettle, in order to prevent the placenta from adhering to the uterus. It is believed that the placenta will adhere to the womb also if anyone walks behind the mother after the seventh month of pregnancy. If both husband and wife are dark in color, the pregnant woman is encouraged to drink the fistula of the Cassia plant dissolved in boiled milk; this is believed to purify the fetus so that the child will be born "almost white."

As soon as the first labor pains are felt, the woman or the midwife takes an image of Saint Raymond and places it upside down with a candle burning in front of it. As soon as the baby is born, the saint is restored to the upright position, but the candle may remain burning for a while. The mother strictly observes forty days of confinement after the birth, during which time fresh air is excluded from her room as much as possible, and her ears are plugged with cotton. No one who has been exposed to the night air or the moonlight may

HEALTH CARE

Theoretically, all citizens are entitled to free health care in the Dominican Republic. Hospitals are free and are staffed by well-trained professionals. However, for the poor, the truth is a different reality. "Free" doesn't include many out-of-pocket expenses; this often makes medical care beyond the means of many people. There are far too few hospitals, and those few are greatly overburdened.

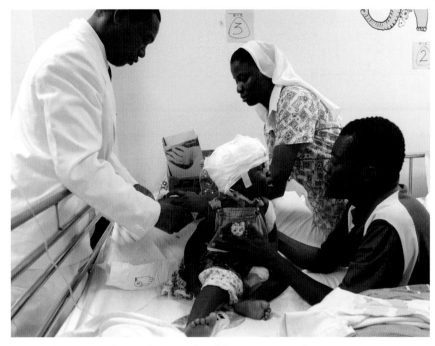

The majority of Dominicans live in unsanitary conditions with inadequate health services and poor nutrition. Health care tends to lack national coordination and management and receives very little money from the government. Consequently, infectious and parasitic diseases are common. Many Dominicans in rural areas rely on home remedies and traditional healers for their medical care.

enter her room for fear of causing her to suffer from *pasmo* (PAHS-moh), a term loosely applied to many illnesses, including tetanus and puerperal fever.

The mother does not nurse the baby for the first three days. She feeds the baby with a decoction made from dried rose petals with a drop of almond oil. Nor does she clip the baby's fingernails until the baby is baptized, or, it is believed, the baby will grow into a thief. The umbilical cord is kept until the child is seven years old; it is then given to the child, who must cut it lengthwise with a knife, to open the ways of life.

Dominican boys harvest coffee in loma de Polo.

GROWING UP

Dominican children often draw their playmates and friends from a large pool of cousins and siblings. Since members of the extended family often live close to one another, cousins play together as closely as brothers and sisters. In Dominican society, parents consider it very important to give birth to at least one son, and many discipline their sons less strictly than their daughters. Girls are closely chaperoned by the whole family, and their brothers and male cousins are expected to protect them and their reputations.

Many children, both in the countryside and in the cities, must work to supplement the family's income. Poor children bear heavy responsibility and have little time for fun and games. Campesino girls help their mothers cook and clean, while boys work beside their fathers in the fields.

Children of wealthy families are closely supervised. After school, they may engage in formal lessons, such as art or piano, or play organized sports or informal games. Boys start playing baseball almost as soon as they can walk, and they join local baseball teams when they are six or seven years old. Wealthy parents may send their older children to private college preparatory or high schools in the United States.

In wealthier families, girls often celebrate their fifteenth birthday, or *quinciñera* (keen-see-NYAY-rah), with a large party. Although not as formal in the Dominican Republic as in some Latin American countries, the custom still signifies the girl's transition to adulthood. Less common in recent years, the *quinciñera* is increasingly being replaced by a social celebration at age sixteen, when the girl makes her debut as a woman in Dominican society.

Young Dominicans love going out at night in large groups. In the big cities, they go to the movies and dance clubs, eat ice cream, or just spend time together gossiping, flirting, driving up and down the main avenue, and generally having a good time. More conservative parents do not allow their children, especially their daughters, to go on dates without a chaperon. Many couples, or *novios* (NOH-byohs), date in groups, with friends who can act as chaperons. Young women pay a lot of attention to their appearance, venturing out in dresses and high heels, and with carefully coifed hair and decorative jewelry. Young men dress in style as well and liberally spray themselves with cologne. They guard the behavior of their girlfriends and sisters jealously, but they flirt animatedly with other girls.

Young baseball players show their spirit.

Many Dominicans follow the Spanish custom of having a double surname, taking the patrimonial surname from both parents to form their own surname. A noted Dominican literary family provides a good example of the patrilineal distribution of family names. Dominican poet Nicolás Ureña de Mendoza had three names: Nicolás was his first name; Ureña was his father's surname, which he also passed on to his children; and de Mendoza was his mother's surname, which his children did not inherit. His daughter, poet Salomé Ureña, married journalist and politician Francisco Henríquez y Carvajal, becoming Salomé Ureña de Henríquez. Their sons, named Pedro Henríquez Ureña and Max Henríquez Ureña, became distinguished literary critics and historians.

GENDER ROLES

Gender roles in the Dominican Republic tend to be defined by the concept of machismo, or masculine pride. Men are often concerned with conforming to a macho image. They strive to appear strong and domineering, but are rather conscious of how they appear when others are looking. They may try to reinforce their macho image and self-image by maintaining a strong camaraderie with other men and by making comments to passing females.

Machismo is also characterized by masculine appeal, so that many Dominican men carry on romantic affairs outside their marriages. Moreover, there is no shame for a man to have children out of wedlock as long as he takes responsibility for them. Machismo also dictates that a man should be the head of the family and support his children, whether married or not.

Women, on the other hand, are expected to be docile, protected, virtuous, and submissive. Nonetheless, more and more women are working outside the home, and women head a large number of families, as many fathers are not around or have limited economic assets. An increasing number of women have also started entering politics.

Traditional gender roles are introduced at an early age and reinforced on a daily basis as children grow up. Among the poor, little boys are often allowed to run around naked and play unsupervised in large groups of friends. When they grow up, they are expected to have premarital and extramarital affairs, but girls are carefully groomed and closely chaperoned, and they are expected to be quiet and helpful and, most of all, to stay virtuous before and during marriage.

Mothers are greatly revered in the Dominican Republic, and the mother-child relationship is generally considered pure and indestructible. Mothers are openly affectionate with their children. Fathers, on the other hand, are generally more removed from day-to-day family affairs. They are seen as authority figures to be obeyed and respected without question.

MARRIAGE AND FAMILY

The ideal Dominican marriage process involves a man asking a virtuous young woman to marry him. They have a formal engagement followed by a religious wedding in a lavishly decorated church, which concludes with an elaborate fiesta, attended by throngs of relatives and friends. In modern Dominican society, this ideal, if realized at all, is generally reserved for the middle and upper classes. The frequency of free unions, or common-law marriages, demonstrates that the ideal marriage process usually involves resources that poor Dominicans cannot afford.

There are three types of long-term union in the Dominican Republic: civil, religious, and common-law marriages. Close to 80 percent of young Dominicans join in free unions, and approximately half of them break up while still in their twenties. Upon dissolution of a free union, the only property that the woman receives is the house, if the couple owned one. She may receive child support only if the father legally recognizes the children. Most poor Dominicans cannot afford to marry officially, especially when they are young. Many of them later marry someone in a civil or religious ceremony, however, if they have a bit more economic security.

A young couple kisses during their wedding ceremony.

Civil marriages performed by the state are the most common. This is probably because annulments are very difficult and expensive to obtain through the Roman Catholic Church, while divorce is relatively easy to obtain from the government.

Kinship ties, extended through the system of godparents, constitute a major source of political and economic power in Dominican society. Parents choose the godparents, or *compadres* (kom-PAH-drays), a few months before the birth of their child. The selection depends not only on the character and friendship of the godparents-to-be but on their financial situation as well. The *compadres* are not only to guide the child spiritually but also to help him or her economically. They are expected to assist in paying for the baptism ceremony and celebration, and often assume financial responsibility for the child's education, medical care, marriage, and even funeral. Throughout his or her life, a godchild has the right to ask his or her *compadres* for financial aid.

The godparents treat their godchild with great affection, often to the extent of tolerating mischief and hiding misbehavior from the parents, especially if the child is a boy. In turn, the child treats the godparents with a mixture of respect and affection.

The parents and the godparents also share a special relationship, treating each other with extreme reverence and formality, even if they were very close friends before the child's baptism.

EDUCATION

In 2014, 91.8 percent of the Dominican population was literate, a tremendous increase from 74 percent of the population in 1986. The Secretariat of State for Education and Welfare administers the system of education and requires Dominican children to attend at least six years of primary school, beginning at age seven. In rural areas, however, not all schools offer all six grades to their communities. Preschool education is available in some areas but is not compulsory.

Secondary education is not compulsory either, and only about two-thirds of the population attend, beginning at age thirteen. Most of those who continue their education beyond secondary school train for university admission, and some attend teacher-training, polytechnic, or vocational schools. Many of the secondary educational programs suffer from low academic standards and high drop-out rates. Most students are required to buy their own textbooks, which dissuades many from enrolling. Many urban middle-class families send their children to private secondary schools, most of which are operated by the Roman Catholic Church.

There are eight universities and a total of more than 26 institutions of higher education in the Dominican Republic. Many wealthy families send their children to schools in the United States.

The Dominican Republic's only public university is the Autonomous University of Santo Domingo (UASD). It traces its roots directly to the Universitas Santi Dominici, which the Spanish established in 1538 as the first university in the Americas. The UASD has for decades been the hub of student

Children work at computers in a renovated school in 2014.

Overcrowded buses and vans tear through the streets of Santo Domingo or, alternatively, crawl along in its heavy traffic. Since the fares on these conveyances are relatively low, the majority of Dominicans in the city use them to go back and forth to work and to do their shopping. On special occasions, those who can afford it might take a taxi. Only wealthy Dominicans can afford to own a car.

Santo Domingo is the hub of a transportation system that carries people and goods to almost anywhere in the country. Most goods are transported by truck to the major market centers, although a government-owned railroad also carries freight through the eastern half of the Cibao, from La Vega to the port of Sánchez on the Bay of Samaná. In the absence of a passenger railway, people travel by bus or car within the country. The other railroads, publicly and privately owned, primarily serve the sugar industry.

The most common means of transportation in the rural and suburban parts of the Dominican Republic is the motorcycle or riding in the back of a pickup truck.

political activity and government opposition. Whereas the battles of the 1960s concerned human rights, students today focus on budget issues.

The leading private universities include the Catholic University Mother and Teacher (UCMM) and the Pedro Henríquez Ureña National University (UNPHU). The UCMM is administered by the Roman Catholic Church in Santiago. The UNPHU is a technical university in Santo Domingo. These private universities tend to enroll students who are wealthier and less occupied with political issues.

A traditional house is enlivened with bright colors.

HOUSING

The Dominican Republic suffers from an urban housing crisis. Urban development cannot keep up with the level of migration to the cities, condemning thousands of poor Dominicans to makeshift shelters in open lots or abandoned buildings. Rural housing varies from upper-class estates, to the most primitive barracks for sugarcane workers.

RURAL HOUSING Many agricultural plantations hire large numbers of temporary workers for the harvest. The majority of these workers are provided with stark housing. They sleep in overcrowded concrete barracks with no water, electricity, or sewage facilities.

More permanent agricultural workers are often allowed to live on company land in small shacks called *bohíos* (boh-EE-ohs). In the more prosperous Cibao region, houses are built of solid palm board or pine. The occupants paint the houses in unusually bright colors with vividly contrasting shutters and lintels. The roofs are made of simple materials such as sheets of zinc or tin, or they might be thatched in poorer households. Most rural Dominicans live on packed earthen floors, although the better off sometimes have concrete floors.

URBAN HOUSING Squatter settlements are rapidly spreading around the edges of the major cities. People move from smaller towns or from the countryside and establish a tenuous foothold in the urban areas by building a shelter out of whatever materials they can gather, such as cardboard or discarded inner tubes.

Wealthier Dominicans live in modern houses in nice neighborhoods, often protecting their properties with security gates and high walls.

DEATH

If a person becomes seriously ill, close relatives and intimate friends congregate at the patient's house. Most of them stay there day and night until after the funeral or until the person recovers. They relieve the patient's family of all duties and responsibilities by ministering to the patient's needs as well as doing the housework.

As soon as a person is pronounced dead, all receptacles that contain water must be emptied at once. Campesinos believe that the ghost bathes in every available vessel in the house, even in the drinking gourd. They consider it "bad" to use such water. The attendants also shut or block the front door of the house for nine days, or *la novena* (la noh-BAY-nah), during which time one can enter the house only through the back door, even if it means tearing down a fence to get to it.

Finally, the family covers all mirrors or turns them against the wall to prevent anyone from seeing a reflection of the ghost's image, which, they believe, will drive them insane. The family of the deceased crowds into one room with the corpse and remains there until the funeral the next day. They place the corpse in a casket, the feet facing the front of the house, with two candles at each end of the casket.

Close family members sit in the house with the corpse, praying, crying, and singing. They discuss all the good qualities of the deceased, recounting even the smallest good deed. The mourners, especially the women, dress in black or grey. In rural areas, the mourning tends tobe especially intense, often with experienced wailers who utter loud mournful cries and go into hysterical fits at the sight of the corpse. The wailing continues until the corpse is taken out for the funeral.

Outside the house, friends and family gather in support of the mourners. The atmosphere outside is often lighter. People tell stories of the deceased, laugh, eat, tell riddles, and even play dominoes.

At the end of the ninth day of *la novena*, the mourners will hold a ceremony called *la vela de muerto* (la BAY-lah day MOOAIR-toh)—the vigil for the dead. More common among the less educated and in the smaller towns, the ceremony

A cemetery in Montecristi

varies in size and style. In more elaborate versions, the mourners renew their wailing, praying, and singing, and construct a small altar surrounded by one to four candles or lanterns. On the altar, they place a crucifix or a picture of a saint, a small pair of scissors to trim the candles, a small saucer in which to put the candle trimmings, a small receptacle for money offerings, and a glass of water for the ghost. On the first death anniversary, the family and friends commemorate the deceased with a similar ceremony.

INTERNET LINKS

www.dw.com/en/dominican-republic-revamps-failing-education-system/a-17625149
President Danilo Medina is staking his reputation on education reform.

moon.com/2010/01/gender-roles-in-the-dominican-republic
Men and women tend to stick to traditional gender roles.

pulitzercenter.org/reporting/caribbean-dominican-republic-pregnancy-youth-sex-education
Teen pregnancy is a major problem in the Dominican Republic.

RELIGION

AVE MARIA GRATIA PLENA DOMINUS TE CUM
BENEDICTA TU IN MULIERIBUS ET BENEDICTUS FRUCTUS VENTRIS TUI

The Basilica of Our Lady of Altagracia in Higuey is a Catholic cathedral dedicated to the nation's patron saint.

8

W HEN YOU SAY "RELIGION" IN THE Dominican Republic, it usually means just one thing: Catholic. Ninety-five percent of the Dominican population today is Roman Catholic. The remaining five percent are Protestant and a mixture of religious beliefs including Islam, which came to the country with immigrants from the Middle East. An even smaller number are followers of folk religions, such as Voodoo.

The Dominican Republic has one Catholic archdiocese in Santo Domingo and another in Santiago. The church leadership tends to be orthodox in outlook. Many Dominican priests, however, are more liberal, engaging in community development projects and forming "Christian base communities." These are groups of people who practice religious devotions and work to improve poverty conditions.

GROWTH OF THE CHURCH

During the first century after colonization, Dominican friars and other missionary orders were active in Santo Domingo. Not until 1564 did the Vatican establish the archdiocese of Santo Domingo and confer upon its archbishop the title of Primate of the West Indies and of America. The authority of the archbishop unfortunately failed to live up to

The Cathedral of Santa María la Menor in Santo Domingo is the oldest cathedral in the Americas, begun in 1512 and completed in 1540. The remains of Christopher Columbus, who died in Spain in 1506, were moved to the cathedral in 1542, but have since been moved back to Spain.

the illustriousness of his title, due to Santo Domingo's rapidly declining importance within the Spanish colonial system; nor has his stature been enhanced since independence, given the country's relatively minor position in Latin America. The colonial Church nonetheless managed to maintain a certain degree of prestige through the eminence of its university, which was considered to be the most venerable theological center in Spanish America.

The Church in the Dominican Republic lost a great deal of its power during the Haitian occupation. Perceiving the Church as an instrument of colonialism and slavery, the Haitians stripped it of all material assets. Even after independence, it failed to regain its former position. Over the next century, the Church struggled unsuccessfully to regain the right to property ownership, as concessions were granted by one government only to be withdrawn by the following government.

In 1929 only Trujillo's intervention stopped the congress from liquidating all Church property after the Dominican supreme court ruled that the Church had no legal existence. Trujillo used the Church as one of his many instruments of power. Under his rule, the Church became one part of the controlling triumvirate, the other two parts being the armed forces and the oligarchy.

Believing that Spanish priests would be more theologically conservative and more likely to preach obedience to his rule, Trujillo persuaded the

Vatican to send a large contingent of priests from Spain to the Dominican Republic. The alliance between the dictator and the Vatican was sealed with the concordat of 1954. It established Roman Catholicism as the official religion in the Dominican Republic.

The Church often turned a blind eye to Trujillo's abuses of power, with a single exception in 1960, when Church officials protested the mass arrests of government opponents. This so incensed Trujillo that he ordered a campaign of harassment against the Church. Only his assassination prevented his planned imprisonment of the Dominican bishops.

Since the end of the Trujillo dictatorship, the Church's political power has declined, primarily due to a policy of "benign neglect" between the government and the Church.

President Danilo Medina offers an amber rosary to Pope Francis at the Vatican in June 2014.

ROMAN CATHOLICISM

Although many Dominicans are not regular churchgoers, most still mark significant life events with religious ceremonies and regard the parish priest as an important figure in rural society.

Dominicans respect the advice of the clergy concerning religious matters, but not secular matters. Nevertheless, the parish priest is often the only person outside the kinship group in whom Dominicans trust and confide.

Despite its diminished political power, the Church carries a major responsibility for public health care and education. The Church manages hospitals, clinics, pharmacies, orphanages, and convalescent homes, as well as nursery schools, elementary and secondary schools, colleges, vocational and technical institutes, teacher-training colleges, and seminaries.

Catholic bishops have been vocal in demanding government reform with respect to human rights and poverty alleviation. At the parish level, some priests have tried to develop Christian-based communities in order to help people to organize and work together.

The Roman Catholic Church was the primary agent for disseminating Spanish culture in the Americas through its missionaries and teaching.

PROTESTANTISM

The first Protestants came to the Dominican Republic as migrants from North America in the 1820s. Their numbers increased around the turn of the century with the immigration of West Indian laborers. The 1960s and 1970s saw a boom in Dominican Protestantism, as evangelical Protestants successfully proselytized in the rural parts of the country. The primary evangelical groups in the Dominican Republic are the Seventh Day Adventists, the Dominican Evangelical Church, and the Assemblies of God.

Evangelical Protestants emphasize biblical fundamentalism, personal and familial rejuvenation, and economic entrepreneurship. Because services are conducted in a more egalitarian fashion than they are in the hierarchical Roman Catholic Church, poor Dominicans are especially attracted to Protestantism. Evangelical Protestant services are relatively spontaneous, allowing people to talk, sing, or give testimony about their religious experiences.

Tensions have been building between the Catholic Church and evangelical Protestants in the Dominican Republic. Many evangelical Protestants blame the conflict with the Vatican for marginalizing their churches and ministers, because it grants the Catholic Church privileges not accorded to evangelical Protestant Churches.

The faithful celebrate Saint Michael Archangel in the Colonial Zone of Santo Domingo.

Many Dominicans perceive good or bad omens in various occurrences in daily life. There are many omens to do with death. For example, the cooing of wild doves near a house means that someone will die soon in the neighborhood. If an owl screeches near a house or alights on the roof, it announces a death in the family. If all the hens cackle together, a death will occur in the family or in the neighbor's family. Also, a person should avoid sleeping with feet toward the front of the house; a person who does that will die.

Then there are omens to do with money. If a person dreams of excrement, he can expect to receive money. The same goes if the palm of his right hand itches. But if his left palm itches, a forgotten debt will have to be paid, or he will lose money.

Several signs are believed to bring misfortune. Spilling the oil when filling a lamp announces misfortune for the person who spills it. Opening an umbrella inside the house, and sweeping the house at night also cause misfortune.

At night, when a horse tires after covering a relatively short distance, it is a sign that a ghost has been riding behind the rider. The rider should stop as soon as he realizes what is happening, or the ghost will give him the sickness from which the ghost died. To drive the ghost away, the saddle should be reversed, placing its front toward the tail of the horse.

FOLK RELIGION

Approximately one million Dominicans of Haitian descent continue to speak Creole French and celebrate their ancestral Vudu (Voodoo) ceremonies. In the Dominican Republic, followers of voodoo generally practice their religion in secret, because the Dominican government and the general population deride it as pagan and African.

Vudo, or VooDoo, is a pop-culture caricature of Voudon, a religion that developed in Haiti and other parts of the Caribbean with the importation of African slaves. The slaves combined their West African beliefs with the Roman Catholicism of their masters to produce Voudon.

Voudon teaches belief in a supreme god called Bondye, an uninvolved creator god. Voudon believers worship many spirits (called Ioa), each one of whom is responsible for a specific area or part of human life. If you are in love, for instance, you would praise and leave offerings for Erzulie Freda, the Voudon spirit of love. If you are a farmer, or a merchant, or someone else, you would beseech specific gods for good fortune and prosperity, for instance. Voudon believes that the spirits can also possess the bodies of their worshippers. This is a beneficial possession. In a ceremony guided by a priest or priestess, possession is considered a valuable first-hand experience and a direct connection with the spirit world. Dominican Voudon, also known as Las 21 Divisiones, is less strict than Haitian Voudon, with fewer rules and fixed ceremonies. Dominican Voudon practitioners are known by various names, including Mama Mambos and Mama Loa.

While the Dominicans claim that only Haitians practice voodoo, many of them nevertheless believe in the magical powers of voodoo.

Many Dominicans seek advice from *curanderos* (cur-ahn-DAY-rohs), or healers, and *brujos* (BREW-hos), or witch doctors. A *curandero* will often consult the saints to ascertain which herbs, roots, and various home cures to employ in their healing arts. The powers of the *brujo* are slightly more dramatic, since he can drive out possessive spirits that sometimes seize an individual. Dominicans consider *brujos* and *curanderos* intermediaries to God.

Some Dominicans also use certain prayers almost as incantations. Among the campesinos and the urban lower class, people recite specific prayers—generally to Jesus, the Virgin Mary, or a saint—in supplication for protection against evil or sometimes as formulas to cure specific diseases. A person might know one or two such prayers, which he or she believes to be a very powerful defence against evil spirits or against failure in any undertaking. Many Dominicans carry a copy of a favorite prayer as an amulet.

Incantations that are believed to be endowed with healing powers are called *ensalmos* (ehn-SAL-mohs). Folk healers use *ensalmos* like prescriptions for diagnosed illnesses—there are specific *ensalmos* for specific maladies. If someone faints, for example, a folk healer may whisper one such incantation in the person's ear.

INTERNET LINKS

cronkite.asu.edu/buffett/dr/religion.html
Jesuits champion social justice in the Dominican Republic today.

www.livescience.com/40803-voodoo-facts.html
Separate the facts from the myths about Voodoo.

www.sacred-destinations.com/dominican-republic/santo-domingo-cathedral
Take a look at the oldest cathedral in the Americas, in Santo Domingo.

LANGUAGE

Colorful street signs attract shoppers on Durante Avenue in the Colonial Zone, the old section of Santo Domingo.

9

THE OVERWHELMING MAJORITY of Dominicans speak Spanish, the official language of the Dominican Republic. As inhabitants of the first Spanish colony in the Americas, Dominicans take pride in speaking a clear, almost classical Spanish, just as they pride themselves on having the purest Spanish traditions in all of Latin America.

Dominican Spanish closely resembles the Castilian Spanish spoken in most of Spain. Differences in pronunciation derive from differences in the way the language has evolved on either side of the Atlantic Ocean since colonial times. For example, the soft c sound and the z are pronounced as a soft th (as in think) in most of contemporary Spain, whereas Dominicans pronounce the soft c and the z as an s.

English has influenced the Dominican language to a certain degree, mainly through the preponderance of Dominicans with family members and friends in the United States. Dominicans living in the United States, especially the so-called Dom-Yorks in New York City, take pride in their bilingual abilities and in their knowledge of US culture.

TAINO/ARAWAK INFLUENCES

The Spaniards adopted several Taino/Arawak words. Many of these were subsequently absorbed into English. Words such as cassava, potato, tobacco, hammock, hurricane, and canoe are derived from the classical

Dominicans tend to talk very quickly and loudly. However, they also communicate silently using facial gestures such as puckered lips and nose twitching. If people don't hear or understand someone talking to them, they might wrinkle their nose—as if their nose is itchy—to mean "what?"

Spanish phonetic spellings of the Taino/Arawak words cazabe (KAH-sah-bay), patata (pah-TAH-tah), tabaco (tah-BAH-koh), hamaca (AH-mah-kah), huracán (uhr-ah-KAHN), and canoa (kahn-OH-ah). The list testifies to the impact of Amerindian products on European culture. The Spaniards also adopted geographical names such as cibao, or plain, and bani, or abundance of water. The city Higüey was named for one of the Taino/Arawak regional groups in the southeast.

AFRICAN INFLUENCES

One of the oldest and most pervasive elements of Dominican culture is the concept of the fucú. African slaves brought the word with them to the island, although its exact origin in Africa is unknown.

A *fucú* is something of ill omen that is likely to bring bad luck; it can also describe something of doom in a person, a place, or an event. At the materialization of a *fucú* in any form, Dominicans will sign a cross in the air with their index fingers and exclaim "¡*Zafa!*" (SAH-fah)—a verbal remedy to any curse the *fucú* might inflict upon them. The word *zafa* was also introduced by African slaves.

A street vendor reads a newspaper as he waits for customers.

RIDDLES

Although declining in frequency, riddling still constitutes an enjoyable pastime in the smaller towns and rural areas of the Dominican Republic. When campesinos gather for wakes, weddings, or other social occasions, they may start telling riddles after exhausting the various topics of conversation. Someone starts the process by offering the first riddle to the group, in a playfully challenging attitude. The group responds with a great deal of comment and criticism before answering or, if it is a new riddle unknown to them, giving up. After that, everyone comments on the riddle again and jokes about it in light of its interpretation. Then someone else follows

Christopher Columbus is considered a national hero, but Dominicans have for centuries considered the utterance of his name to be bad luck. Instead of actually speaking his name, many Dominicans insist on referring to him indirectly as "the Admiral" or "the Discoverer." One commits a fucú (foo-KU), or invites bad luck, by calling him by name. It is common to use his name as an all-purpose expletive. Dominicans exclaim "¡Colón!" (Columbus's Spanish name) much in the same fashion that they might cry out "¡Ay, Dios!"

Propaganda for the quincentenary, or 500th anniversary celebration of Columbus's arrival in the Americas, tried with limited success to drown out the superstition regarding the explorer's name. When the Columbus Lighthouse was finally turned on, many Dominicans prayed that they would not be cursed; some government officials even refused to attend the lighthouse's inauguration. It has been said that the fucú cursed aspects of the lighthouse construction, including the crashing in 1937 of three airplanes—named for Columbus's ships the Niña, the Pinta, and the Santa María—in a fundraising flight for the lighthouse.

There are many more bizarre incidents that have served to convince Dominicans of all classes that the fucú

The Mausoleum of Christopher Columbus inside the Columbus Lighthouse

is legitimate. In the 1940s a politician was pricked by a medal when he was awarded the Order of Columbus; the politician died when the wound became infected. In 1946, at a ceremony marking the 450th anniversary of Santo Domingo's founding, an earthquake struck when Columbus's urn was opened.

up with perhaps another riddle with the same answer, or with a new and different riddle.

The content of many of the riddles concern everyday objects, such as avocados, honeybees, needles, or garlic. Some riddles suggest sexual concepts either obliquely or overtly. Riddles that merely suggest sexual ideas but then give inoffensive answers may be recited in front of women, but it is considered improper for women to recite them.

The riddle is distinguished by how eloquently the speaker poses it, so that it works not only as a puzzle to be solved, but also so that it has artistic merit. Sometimes the riddles are offered in poetic verse.

DOMINICAN SAYINGS AND EXPRESSIONS

Dominicans demonstrate their renowned friendliness with a gracious welcome to anyone who enters their home. Visitors are greeted with the traditional expression *"Mi casa, su casa"* (mee kah-sah, soo kah-sah), meaning "my house is your house."

Several sayings and expressions, or *dichos* (DEE-chohs), describe the relation of skin color to class and political power. Examples are "colonels are never black" (even if their skin is dark), "money whitens," and "a rich black is a mulatto, a rich mulatto is a white man." However, Dominicans also make light of their color-consciousness, with *dichos* such as "we all have a little black behind the ears." (However, one may note how those sayings all disparage blackness. Indeed, despite the fact that 90 percent of Dominicans have some degree of African descent, in general they tend to see those African roots as shameful.)

Some Dominican sayings derive from a Spanish heritage. For example, "no Moors on the coast" means figuratively "the coast is clear." The expression refers to the centuries-long war between medieval Spain and the Islamic Moors, and it also suggests the Dominican resentment of Haiti's occupation in the nineteenth century. Another Spanish saying that is also common in the Dominican Republic is "the Devil is wise more because he is old than because he is the Devil," signifying that wisdom comes with age or experience. Certain proverbs and sayings carry the flavor of their rural origins. "While the dog

RIDDLE ME THIS

Riddle: *White I leave my house.*
            Green was my birth.
            With the maturation of time
            White I return to my house.

Answer: Garlic

Riddle: *The one who makes it does not use it.*
            The one who uses it does not see it.
            The one who sees it does not desire it
            no matter how pretty it may be.

Answer: *A coffin*

is skinniest, he has the most fleas" signifies that misfortune continues to plague the person who is already suffering. Another folk saying, "one can always find a hair in the *sancocho* (san-KOH-choh)," or stew, means that good things are never perfect. The pragmatic nature of the Dominican campesino is demonstrated by the proverb "better to say 'from here I fled' than 'here I died.'"

INTERNET LINKS

www.bigorrin.org/archive75.htm
Taino/Arawak words that influenced Dominican Spanish are listed here.

www.colonialzone-dr.com/language-sayings.html
This site offers a long list of Dominican sayings in Spanish with English explanations.

www.dominicanrepublicrealestate.ca/fact-sheet/dominican-republic-spanish-dialect/
Here, find some characteristics of Dominican Spanish.

ARTS

Souvenir maracas are offered for sale to tourists. Maracas are wooden percussion instruments that can accompany a merengue.

DOMINICANS ARE A COLORFUL AND joyful and expressive people in all areas. Not surprisingly, they have contributed greatly in all areas of the arts from music, to poetry, to literature, and painting. The *merengue* (mer-REN-gay) is a type of music and dance that was invented on Hispaniola, and is now popular all over the world, especially in Latin America. Dominican contributions to both literature and painting aren't as famous, but they both show the Dominican love of life and its celebrations.

WRITERS AND POETS

The most significant writer of the colonial period was Bartolomé de Las Casas. Las Casas recorded the early history of the Caribbean area in his *Historía de las Indias*, which remains one of the most important historical records of the Spanish conquest of the Americas and the indigenous peoples of the Caribbean.

Dominican literature developed during the Romantic era in France, and that style's influence persisted in the Dominican Republic through the nineteenth century. The outstanding work of that period was the

This mural by Constantino Brumidi shows the Spanish friar Bartolomé de las Casas with the Taino Cacique hero Enriquillo.

classic Dominican novel *Enriquillo*, published in 1882, by Manuel de Jesús Galván (1834—1910). Exemplifying the Romantic ideal of "the noble savage," *Enriquillo* stands out as a masterpiece of Spanish-American literature. In 1954 Robert Graves translated Galván's novel into English with the title *The Cross and the Sword*.

A leading contemporary of Galván was Salomé Ureña de Henríquez (1850—1896), a schoolteacher who wrote poetry filled with patriotic fervor about political themes of the day. Much of her poetry was intensely personal in style.

The evolution from romanticism to realism and then to modernism took only a decade in the Dominican Republic. Gastón Fernando Deligne (1861—1912) led the modernist movement. Inspired by Nicaragua's Rubén Darío, Deligne aspired to modernist symbolism, declaring that "to write poetry is to turn ideas into images."

Another literary movement of the early twentieth century was *postumismo* (pohs-too-MEES-moh), which attempted to establish a new style of poetry and prose by casting off Spanish and early Dominican influences. Domingo Moreno Jimenes (1894—1986) exemplifies *postumismo* in his work *Palabras en el Agua* ("*Words on Water*"). The poetry presents images floating and jostling each other in the current of incessant change.

A recent literary movement, *poesía de sorpresa* (poh-AYS-EEYA day sor-PRAY-sah), or "surprise poetry," has developed out of the *postumismo* movement. *Poesía de sorpresa* utilizes imagery deliberately chosen for its shock effect. Héctor Incháustegui Cabral (1912—1979) led the *poesía de sorpresa* movement with works such as *El Miedo en un Puñado de Polvo* ("*Fear in a Handful of Dust*"). This dramatic trilogy in verse draws its themes from Greek tragedy and its style from T. S. Eliot.

Julia Alvarez (b. 1950) is a poet and novelist who writes about "Dom-Yorks," Dominican New Yorkers who live between two cultures, American and Dominican. Born in New York, she left the United States at age three and spent the next ten years in the Dominican Republic until her father's involvement in a plot to overthrow the Trujillo dictatorship forced the family to move back to the United States.

Now a college professor, Alvarez's best-known novel is In the Time of the Butterflies *(1995), about repression under Trujillo. It was made into a movie starring Salma Hayek in 2001. Some of her other notable novels are* How the Garcia Girls Lost Their Accents, A Gift of Gracias, *and* A Wedding in Haiti. *She received the US National Medal of Arts in 2014.*

Former President Juan Bosch (he served for less than a year in 1963) is also known for several novels and short stories, the best of which are collected in two volumes of short stories, *Cuentos Escritos en el Exilio* ("Stories Written in Exile") and *Más Cuentos Escritos en el Exilio* ("More Stories Written in Exile"). He has also written several political polemics, as well as a history of his aborted presidency, *Crisis of Democracy of America in the Dominican Republic.*

MUSICIANS

The most famous kind of Dominican music and dance is the merengue,
which Dominicans share with Haitians. The merengue combines the Spanish
pasodoble (pah-soh-DOH-blay), or two-step, with the African tom-tom.
Originally a rural folk dance and later a ballroom dance, the merengue is
danced with a limping step, the weight always on the same foot. It is said
to have been first danced by a crippled general whose guests respectfully
imitated his movements as he dragged his lame right leg across the floor.
Couples dance, in casual or traditional dress, with limping steps to rhythmic
lyrics that comment on love, politics, destiny, or even illegal emigration to
the United States.

Peasant farmers developed the merengue and turned it into a national
obsession. In the city, the merengue music gushes from taxis, self-service
stores, bars, restaurants, and even fast-food outlets. Merengue serves as the
background music for everyday Dominican life. In the evening, it turns the

THE ART OF AUDIENCE PARTICIPATION

As with most Caribbean forms of live music and dance performances, the merengue depends upon group participation. There is no division between active performers and a passive audience. While certain gifted instrumentalists or singers might dominate certain segments of the performance, members of the audience are expected to participate by clapping, offering encouragement, or even dancing themselves. In fact, the more enthusiastically the audience participates, the more successful the performance becomes. The exchange develops into a circular process, in which the leading musicians and singers are spurred on to greater degrees of musical execution by higher and higher levels of audience participation.

Merengue lyrics are noted for their social commentary on love and politics. They are often ironic, humorous, clever, critical, and even a bit scandalous. Others comment on issues of everyday life. A contemporary merengue song, by Wilfredo Vargas, says:

"Puerto Rico queda cerca, pero móntate en avión,
y si consigues la visa, no hay problema en Inmigración.
Pero no te vayas en yola, no te llenes de ilusiones,
porque en el Canal de la Mona, te comen los tiburones."

"Puerto Rico is close by, but get yourself on a plane,
and if you can get a visa, no problem in immigration.
But don't you go by yola, don't let your dreams delude you,
because in the Mona Passage, the sharks will surely eat you."

waterfront of Santo Domingo into an open-air gala, warmly pulsating with noise, music, people, lights, and cars.

A special merengue festival takes place in Santo Domingo in the last week of July. All along the waterfront, Dominicans and thousands of tourists from Puerto Rico and Western Europe celebrate the merengue with all-night partying.

The guitar is probably the most popular musical instrument in the Dominican Republic. In some rural areas, musicians also commonly play flutes and homemade marimbas. Merengue music is played on locally made percussion instruments, such as the *tambora* (tahm-BOH-rah) and the *guiro* (goo-EER-oh), although high-tech synthesizers are sometimes used instead. By rubbing the *guiro* with a shell or with wire, the musician produces the rasping noise behind the merengue rhythm.

Spanish bolero music and dance are quite popular in the Dominican Republic, as is salsa music. If the merengue expresses the natural vivacity of Dominicans, their pathos is expressed through mournfully romantic *bachata* (bah-chah-tah) ballads. Young Dominicans also enjoy reggae and other modern African-American music, as well as rock music.

Some regions have preserved folkloric dances that are more heavily European in style. In the south, the *mangulina* (mahn-goo-LEE-nah) is commemorated at patron saints' day festivals, as is *la jacana* (la ha-KAH-nah) in the north. These types of ceremonial dances, with Spanish and Taino Arawak origins, form part of the Dominican Republic's folkloric tradition but are not part of the popular culture. Another type of music derived from Spain, which has been preserved in the northern region, consists of ancient vocal choruses known as *salves* (SAHL-vays) and *tonadas* (toh-NAH-dahs).

Dominican composers did without established orchestras until Trujillo created the National Conservatory of Music and Speech in 1941. That year Dominican composers created twenty important musical works.

PAINTERS

Painters in the Dominican Republic have not developed a uniquely Dominican style, although the country has produced many fine painters. Several have achieved notice in Europe and the United States, including Guillo Pérez, Gilberto Hernández Ortega, Ada Balcácer, and Abelardo Urdaneta. While they portray common Dominican themes, they generally do not share a distinctly Dominican mode of expression.

The most prominent style of Dominican painting during the twentieth century was *costumbrismo* (kohs-toom-BREES-moh), which portrays Dominican customs and themes. Urdaneta was a precursor of *costumbrismo*, while Pérez has continued to develop it within a realistic style. Pérez was

famous for portraying sugarcane fields and oxen driven along rutted wagon trails. Later in his career, and in keeping with his reputation for masterful use of color, he concentrated on depicting roosters.

The foremost Dominican painter of recent times is the master Ramón Oviedo (1927—2015). His work documented Dominican life and politics, and his work is exhibited worldwide.

FOLK ARTS AND CRAFTS

Dominican arts and crafts have recently experienced a resurgence throughout the country. The renewed interest is partly due to a collective search for cultural roots among modern-day Dominicans and partly due to encouragement from the government and international development agencies, which see the crafts as a beneficial means of lowering the unemployment rate. Women artisans especially have gained prominence in the revival of traditional Dominican crafts.

Amber and larimar are extremely popular materials, especially in the making of jewelry. Early humans believed that amber captured the sun's rays, and it has been prized for centuries for its beauty and ease of carving.

Amber is a translucent fossil formed from pine tree sap that hardened over millions of years under the weight of layers of soil and ice. Sometimes, the sap trapped organic materials, such as insects, lizards, and flowers, perfectly preserving its silent victims.

Clear amber is popular in jewelry, but scientists greatly value amber with imprisoned fossils, from which they can retrieve DNA material. In 1989 a piece of Dominican amber conclusively proved that mushrooms were 40 million years old, twice as old as previously believed.

The Baltic region traditionally has been the world's primary source of amber, but the Dominican Republic holds some of the largest reserves in the world, as well as some of the most colorful specimens of the gem. Although primarily yellow, orange, or brown, Dominican amber also comes in red, green, blue, and even purple.

Found only in the Dominican Republic, larimar is a semiprecious Dominican stone that is unique because its blue tones vary from deep sky blue to blue green—the result of contact with copper and cobalt oxide during its geological formation. When the larimar deposits on the southern coast were discovered in 1974, Dominicans believed that the stone came from the sea. In actuality, the rivers washed the stones down from the mountain tops and deposited them near the ocean to be naturally polished by the water. One of the first commercial suppliers of the gem named it after his daughter Lari and the sea, el mar (ehl mahr). Today, miners excavate the stone by hand in open pits near Sierra de Bahoruco.

Campesinos in the Cibao region carefully preserve a rich tradition of pottery for household use and a creative art. Decorative ceramics include the production of lamp bases, vases, ashtrays, nativity scenes, ornamental plates, candle holders, and dolls.

Other popular crafts include palm weaving, woodcarving, leatherwork, doll making, and jewelry making. Weavers in various parts of the country use local fibers, including various types of palm leaves, to make baskets, hats, hammock ties, and floor mats and rugs. Artisans also craft popular jewelry from amber, larimar, seashells, tortoiseshell, bone, and coral.

The community of Salcedo produces decoratively carved products from *higuero* (ee-GOOAIR-oh), or calabash, such as lacquered purses, rounded mulatto faces, fish, Spanish maracas, and *guiros*, a merengue instrument. *Guiros* are elongated calabash gourds that the artisan dries and empties through a small hole before carving transverse grooves on the shell. Maracas, used to accompany Spanish music, are dried and hollowed gourds with numerous small seeds inside that make a rasping sound when the gourds are shaken.

Tourists display some clay folk mask souvenirs in the resort area of Punta Cana.

INTERNET LINKS

www.heritageinstitute.com/danceinfo/descriptions/merengue.htm
Read an excellent article about merengue, the national dance of the Dominican Republic.

www.juliaalvarez.com
This is the website of Dominican-American writer Julia Alvarez.

www.thatsdominican.com/dr/press/top-10-dominican-artists
This article offers a list of favorite Dominican musicians.

LEISURE

A teen boy poses with a basketball on his head.

11

DOMINICANS WORK HARD, NOT always from choice, so when some time off comes, they put all their energy into have fun and celebrating life, family, and friendship. In small towns, people gather on the plaza on Sunday after church to visit with friends. The women and children usually go home early to prepare dinner; the men stay and chat, perhaps watch a cockfight, or watch baseball. In small towns or large, storytelling is an age-old Dominican tradition that still captivates young and old in today's age of video games and smart phones.

SPORTS

The most popular team sports in the Dominican Republic are baseball, soccer, volleyball, and basketball. Soccer's following in the country, though active, is small in relation to that in most of Latin America, but baseball is the national passion of the Dominican Republic, fueled by competition in the Caribbean and close contact with North American professional teams.

"If you ask any Dominican what he is proudest of, he will read you a list of ballplayers. This country doesn't have much, but we know we are the best in the world at one thing. That's not bragging, because it's true. And we plan to continue being the best in the world at it."

—Manuel Mota, former outfielder for the Los Angeles Dodgers

In 1974 Santo Domingo hosted the Twelfth Central American and Caribbean Olympic Games, in which approximately 4,000 athletes participated. For the event, the Dominican government constructed an array of facilities, including a large sports palace with a seating capacity of 10,000 spectators, an Olympic-sized swimming pool, a bicycle track, and a shooting range.

BASEBALL Among organized sports, baseball inspires the most national enthusiasm. The Dominican Republic exports more professional baseball players to the United States than does any other country, while major league players from the United States often spend their winters in the Dominican Republic, playing in the professional leagues there. The baseball season begins after the World Series in the United States and runs from October through January.

Children play basketball in the old section of Santo Domingo.

Dominicans start playing baseball almost as soon as they can walk, practicing with old broomsticks and hollowed-out coconut husks for bases. They share gloves and bats between teams, but always play with the high-level intensity that characterizes Dominican baseball. They concentrate on simply throwing, hitting, and running, without coaches, uniforms, or warm-ups. Men continue to play either among themselvesor on organized amateur teams. Those who show talent can reasonably hope that they will be drafted by a professional team in the Caribbean, Canada, or the United States.

It was the Cubans, rather than the US Marines as many people believe, who brought baseball to the Dominican Republic. The Cubans learned the game from US troops stationed in Cuba in the 1860s. The fact that baseball originated in the United States did influence its popularity, however. Starting out as an amateur sport, the game was organized professionally in the

1920s and 1930s, during which time Dominican players gained international recognition for their talent and skill. Furthermore, several legendary US baseball players, including Satchel Paige, were lured away from the segregated Negro League to play for Dominican teams in the heated season of 1937.

Dominican baseball declined after that, though it maintained an avid following at the amateur level, bolstered by play in the sugarcane fields during the slack harvest period. Plantation and refinery managers and owners encouraged employees to play as a diversion in slow times. The game developed a distinctly Dominican flavor, characterized by a close-knit bond between players and their passionate fans.

Professional baseball re-emerged in the Dominican Republic during the 1950s, and US teams began recruiting Dominicans. Amateur play had matured to such an extent that professional teams could draw from amateur teams.

By 2015 there were 83 Dominican baseball players in the major leagues, leading all other countries outside the United States. Their successes encouraged the signing of more professional contracts for Dominicans, who continue to contribute to US baseball history.

COCKFIGHTING

Many Dominican men, especially in the rural areas, remain enthusiastic about cockfighting, although the authorities have tried to suppress interest in this brutal spectator sport. Introduced by the Spaniards, it often provokes criticism from foreign visitors, who charge that it is inherently cruel to the birds. Before the US occupation in 1916, cockfighting was the national pastime, but it has given way to baseball.

Popularized in ancient Rome, cockfighting is an amateur sporting event in which the owners of gamecocks, or *gallos* (GAH-yohs), put their birds in a circular ring about 20 feet (6.1 m) in diameter and let them fight, sometimes to the death. The owners breed and train their gallos especially for fighting, which the birds begin between ages one and two. The birds are equipped with metal or bone spurs averaging about 1.5 inches (3.8 cm) in length, to enhance their ability to hurt their opponents.

At a cockfighting arena in Santo Domingo on a Sunday afternoon, roosters prepare to fight.

After fitting the artificial spurs over the gamecocks' natural spurs, the handlers put the birds into the ring at the same time. The birds become infuriated at the proximity of the other bird or birds and will run and jump at them, trying to spur and wound them in the eyes or chest. On occasion, if one of the birds refuses to fight any longer, the handler will put it breast to breast with the other bird. If the *gallo* still refuses to fight, the judge will rule that it has quit, and the fight ends.

URBAN NIGHTLIFE

Santo Domingo comes alive at night. The middle and upper classes dress up elegantly—women elaborately made-up in dresses and high-heels, and men in ties, slicked-back hair, and cologne. They throng to the city's many restaurants, nightclubs, and casinos, where they eat, drink, and dance to merengue and salsa music until the early hours of the morning.

Since many people cannot afford to enter the expensive nightclubs, however, it is becoming increasingly common for individuals to set up their stereos and large speakers on the sidewalks of the city, creating an atmosphere of cacophonous partying. In the evening, Santo Domingo's waterfront, the

Malecón, is transformed into a narrow, 3-mile-long (5-km-long) street party, filled with cars, pedestrians, dancers, music, and jubilant noise.

ORAL TRADITION

With increasing access to television, storytelling and listening to riddles are no longer as popular with Dominicans as in the not-too-distant past. Today the pastimes of storytelling and riddling exist primarily in small towns or on farms, providing entertainment during social gatherings such as wakes or weddings, during the midday siesta, on Sunday afternoons in the park, or while visiting someone's home.

A relatively large body of folktales exists in the Dominican Republic. Most of the tales have European origins, but a few have African parallels. A set of folktales concern the adventures of Juan Bobo, and another cycle of tales involves Buquí and Lapén. Common folktale themes include magical flights, monsters, supernatural beings, and tales of heroism, morality, trickery, and enchantment.

INTERNET LINKS

www.baseball-reference.com/bio/D-R-_born.shtml
Here is a history of all the Dominican players who have played in the Major Leagues.

dominicancult.blogspot.com/2013/09/la-ciguapa-dominican-succubus.html
The folk legend of "La Ciguapa," the Dominican Succubus.

www.nytimes.com/2008/02/13/sports/othersports/13fight.html?pagewanted=all&_r=0
"Dominicans Say Cockfighting Is in Their Blood" is an eye-opening story about this custom.

FESTIVALS

A huge Christmas tree lights up the street in Santo Domingo.

12

THE RHYTHM OF LIFE IN THE Dominican Republic includes a number of national festivals that are wildly looked forward to by a people who love to celebrate. Carnival is the high point of the year. In the Dominican Republic, Carnival coincides with Independence Day celebrations, giving the holiday added significance.

Every town has its own patron saint, and each Roman Catholic saint has an assigned feast day on the calendar. On that day, the town will celebrate its *Fiesta Patronale*, which typically includes music, parades, and prayer. *Día de la Altagracia*, January 21, commemorates the Virgin Mary of Altagracia, the patron saint of the Dominican Republic.

A colorfully costumed woman parades in the Punta Cana Carnival in 2015.

CALENDAR OF EVENTS

January 1	*New Year's Day*
January 6	*Epiphany*
January 21	*Our Lady of Altagracia*
January 26	*Duarte's Birthday*
February 27	*Independence Day*
Variable	*Carnival*
Variable	*Good Friday*
May 1	*Labor Day*
Variable	*Corpus Christi*
August 16	*Restoration Day*
September 24	*Our Lady of las Mercedes*
November 6	*Constitution Day*
December 25	*Christmas Day*

Dominicans used to believe that if a person went to the beach at Easter, they would turn into a fish. Now, Easter is considered the perfect time for a beach holiday.

Dominicans celebrate Christmas throughout the month of December, ending on Three Kings' Day on January 6. Easter may be celebrated religiously or used as an excuse for a trip to the beach.

THE CHRISTMAS SEASON

Dominicans celebrate Christmas throughout the month of December. They have parties every weekend with family, co-workers, and friends. Dominicans who live abroad flock back to their pueblos, or villages, bearing exotic gifts. Real Christmas trees have become more common in recent years, but traditional Dominican Christmas "trees" are really branches. People might paint the branches white or green and then decorate them with miniature straw or ceramic crafts shaped as hats, baskets, angels, and other objects.

On Christmas Eve, the Dominican extended family enjoys a feast of roasted pig. Catholics then attend a midnight Mass. The church is decorated with a *nacimiento* (nah-see-mee-AIN-toh), or nativity scene, with life-sized wooden images of Joseph, the Virgin Mary, and *el Niño Jesús*, or the Baby Jesus, surrounded by horses, sheep, cows, and shepherds. After the Mass, many people return home to party until sun-rise, while teenagers and couples go out dancing. On Christmas day, *el Niño Jesús* bears gifts to children in the Cibao region, while children in Santo Domingo receive gifts from Santa Claus.

A Santa character performs for children in Santo Domingo.

The Christmas season ends with the arrival of the Three Kings on January 6. It is considered a day for children, who sometimes receive additional holiday gifts from visiting relatives.

EASTER

Dominicans no longer celebrate Easter as religiously as in the past. Nevertheless, for religious Catholics, Semana Santa and Easter Sunday are highly ritualistic holidays. In Santo Domingo, parishioners take the wooden images of Jesus Christ from the churches and march through the streets with the images at the head of the procession.

QUINCENTENARY

Dominican leaders spent more than a century planning for the 500th anniversary of Columbus's arrival in the Americas, which was celebrated on Columbus Day, October 12, 1992. The most significant part of the celebration was the Faro a Colón, or Columbus Lighthouse, the construction of which was first discussed in the mid-1800s. Ground was broken under Trujillo in 1948,

The Museum of the Americas and Mausoleum of Admiral Christopher Columbus in Santo Domingo is usually called the Columbus Lighthouse.

however, the actual construction did not begin until 1986.

The monument is a long horizontal cross, half a mile (0.8 km) long, with slanting walls 120 feet (36.6 m) high. The lighthouse throws a cross of light against the sky rather than across the sea. When lit, its 30 billion-candlepower beacon is visible from Puerto Rico, 150 miles (241.4 km) east.

The construction of the Faro a Colón cost an estimated $70 million dollars, although the government insists it cost only $11 million. The expense of building and powering the memorial has caused a great deal of controversy and resentment among Dominicans.

Unfortunately for the organizers of the celebration, the quincentennial anniversary became the target of transatlantic controversy over the legacy of Columbus. Indigenous peoples in the Americas protested that his "discovery" of the Americas resulted in the destruction of whole civilizations; others celebrated the profound ramifications of this unprecedented exchange of cultures, cuisines, technology, and medical knowledge.

CARNIVAL AND INDEPENDENCE DAY

Carnival originated in medieval Europe as the final feasting and merry-making before Lent, the forty days of fasting and penitence that precede Good Friday and Easter. The Dominican Republic's Independence Day always falls close to the beginning of Lent so that independence and Carnival celebrations often coincide on February 27.

African influences embellish Dominican Carnival celebrations, which resemble Carnival celebrations in Rio de Janeiro and New Orleans. Dominicans dress in a colorful array of fantastic masks and costumes, including European and African designs. One Carnival character is the *diablo cojuelo* (dee-AHB-loh kohn-HOOAY-loh), a horned devil that lashes out at bystanders with inflated cow bladders to purge them of sin. Anthropologists from the Museo del Hombre Dominicano in Santo Domingo have traced the *diablo cojuelo* to medieval Europe.

Other Carnival characters include *Roba la Gallina* (ROH-bah la gah-YEE-nah), who dresses as a transvestite and attracts chanting verses from the spectators; *Marimanta* (mah-ree-MAHN-tah), represented by women in white twirling wide skirts; and *la Muerte Enjipe* (lah MOOAIR-tay ain-HEE-pay), men in black suits with painted skeletons, who dance around the *Marimanta*. They form part of a parade of floats and outlandishly costumed marchers from various municipalities, businesses, and clubs. The parade begins in the late afternoon on Independence Day, when the newly elected king and queen of the celebrations arrive on the Malecón, Santo Domingo's waterfront.

A flamboyant *diablo cojuelo* (horned devil) parades during Carnival celebrations on the Malecón.

Hundreds of wooden stalls called *casetas* (cah-SAY-tahs) are set up along the Malecón, selling rum, sodas, beer, sandwiches, fruit, and other snacks. Each *caseta* plays merengue music on its own radio. Hundreds of thousands of spectators line the Malecón during the parade, and the celebration continues all night long with dancing, singing, and partying in the street.

INTERNET LINKS

www.amstardmc.com/blog/easter-in-punta-cana
Some Dominican Easter activities

www.dominicanmasks.com
Read a good article with excellent photos about Carnival in Santo Domingo.

thingstodo.viator.com/dominican-republic/christmas-in-the-dominican-republic
Christmas in the Dominican Republic

FOOD

Plantains, or green bananas, are a favorite food throughout the Caribbean.

13

THE DOMINICAN DIET IS AS COLORFUL and spicy as Dominican life itself is. It makes use of rice, tubers and plantains, fish and pork with a wide variety of spices and cooking techniques that produce mouth-watering dishes. One thing is for sure: rich or poor, Dominicans love to eat. Food is a critical part of daily life as well as any celebration or get-together.

A fisherman displays his colorful catch in Boca Chica.

Sancocho, a Caribbean meat stew, is practically the national dish of the Dominican Republic. For everyday fare, it is usually made with beef, but for special occasions, the deluxe version is the *Sancocho de Siete Carnes* ("Seven Meat Stew"). The meats include beef, goat, sausage, pork, chicken, pork ribs, and smoked ham.

The colonization of the Americas brought about a global food exchange that permanently influenced cuisines all over the world. The colonists incorporated into their own diet cassava, sweet potatoes, annatto and allspice, hot peppers, and various kinds of beans and fruit from the Caribbean, as well as tomatoes, potatoes, peanuts, papayas, cacao, and avocados from continental America.

In turn, the colonists brought a wide range of foods from elsewhere in the world: from Europe, vegetables such as onions, leeks, carrots, cabbages, asparagus, and artichokes, which flourished in the Caribbean climate; from Africa, millet, okra, watermelons, ackee, plantains, and bananas; from Oceania, mangoes, taro, and breadfruit; and from India and Indonesia, spices.

Through the centuries of exchange and adaptation, Caribbean cuisine developed its own distinctive character. Rather than percolating from the upper-class diet downward to the campesinos, Caribbean cuisine came from the choicest dishes of the poor to become the colorful diet of the elite.

ESSENTIAL INGREDIENTS

Dominican food is described as *comida criolla* (koh-MEE-dah kree-OH-yah), or creole food. It consists primarily of white rice, black or red beans, plantains, and occasionally meat in the form of pork, goat, or, less often, beef. Dominicans like their food spicy but not excessively hot.

Plantains are popular because they are sweet, plentiful, and cheap. Although they resemble the banana, they are larger, more angular, have thicker skins, and must be cooked before eating. Whereas the banana is high in sugar and low in starch, plantains are high in starch and low in sugar. Similar to a potato in texture, plantains are often sliced and fried. Green plantains may be fried, pounded flat, then refried and seasoned with garlic to make *tostones* (tohs-TOHN-ays), or they may be mashed and fried with onions to make the common breakfast dish *mangu* (MAHN-goo). Cassava, sweet potatoes, taro, and yams, which are cheap and easy to grow, also form part of the campesino diet.

A particular Dominican specialty is *sancocho*, a stew made of chicken or some other meat, cooked with cassava and plantains, and seasoned with pepper, coriander, and a dash of vinegar. *Mondongo* (mohn-DOHN-goh), also popular, is made with tripe.

Tostones are made by frying plantain chips.

Dominicans who can afford it enjoy dishes made with pork or goat. Deep-fried pork or chicken skins are also popular, as are various types of sausage made from beef or pork.

Seafood is plentiful in most parts of the country, but some common species, such as red snapper and grouper, are occasionally toxic. Shark, tuna, salmon, cod, lobster, and shellfish are popular. In Samaná, people like to sweeten seafood with coconut.

BEVERAGES Dominicans drink a wide variety of fruit juices, made from the island's abundant fruit, including tamarindo, níspero, jauga, guava, soursop, pineapple, mango, orange, grapefruit, and papaya. They mix the freshly squeezed juice with ice to make *jugo* (HOO-goh) or whisk the juice with milk and ice to make *batido* (bah-TEE-doh).

Dominicans drink coffee at least three times a day with meals. They might buy juice or coffee from restaurants or street vendors throughout the day.

Dominicans enjoy drinking beer and rum in the evenings and on weekends. These are also the most popular alcoholic beverages during holidays or ceremonial celebrations such as weddings.

A Dominican family prays before a meal.

MEALTIMES

Dominican families eat most of their meals together, even the midday meal, unless one or both parents cannot return from work. The mother often serves everyone at the table, especially in rural families where she wants to make sure that everyone receives a fair portion. In rural households, children generally do not serve themselves at mealtimes. The mother does the serving, and they must clean their plates. In many urban families, however, everyone at the table serves themselves.

BREAKFAST The first meal of the day, *el desayuno* (el day-sai-OON-oh), usually consists of plantains or some type of boiled root, especially in the rural areas, where campesinos need a filling breakfast to start off the day. In the cities, *el desayuno* may consist of cereal or bread with coffee and juice.

LUNCH Lunch is the largest meal of the day and is often followed by a siesta, or rest period. Lunch, or *el almuerzo* (al-moo-AIR-soh), always consists of rice and beans in some form, and may include meat, or perhaps the stew *sancocho*.

Dominicans try to eat *elalmu-er-zo* at home if possible, although many workers must take their lunches to work with them and do not take a siesta. In small towns, all businesses close for a few hours in the middle of the day and open again in the afternoon and into the evening. In the cities, only a minority of businesses observe the siesta. Although government offices do not officially close at lunchtime, public officials are usually unavailable during the midday hours.

SUPPER The evening meal usually consists of a combination of boiled roots, with eggs, bread, spaghetti, mashed potatoes, or perhaps *mangu*. Dominicans love sweet desserts, some of which are made from staples such as beans, plantains, and tubers. They candy sweet potatoes and red beans, and make corn puddings. They also enjoy a variety of rich cakes and the pervasive Hispanic caramel custard, flan.

A street vendor cooks up some fritters and other snacks.

EATING OUT IN SANTO DOMINGO

The country's capital offers a variety of restaurants and international cuisine. In addition to Dominican food, diners have their choice of Italian, French, Chinese, Mexican, and Argentine cuisine, as well as a few vegetarian and fine seafood restaurants.

In the streets, vendors sell snacks of *tostones*, sausages, and *quipes* (KEE-pays), which are fried dumplings filled with meat or cheese. One can also buy fresh juice or sodas, and coffee or espresso.

FEASTS

While any large gathering might provide an excuse for celebration with food and drink, the most common occasions are Christmas Eve, the New Year, Easter, Carnival, and local patron saint's days. Celebrations usually involve

PARTY FOOD AND ETIQUETTE

There are a few points of etiquette to familiarize foreign guests with the Dominican way of partying. An evening party in the Dominican Republic is typically characterized by merengue music and a lot of dancing, and children are involved in the party rather than sent off to play among themselves.

In keeping with the ethos of relaxation, guests should never arrive early or even punctually; they should come a little later than the invitation time to be sure that they are not the first to arrive. Guests should also eat a snack in the early evening before going to the party because even though Dominicans serve lots of food at their gatherings, they tend to do so around or even after midnight. This is because the usual custom is to eat and leave. Hosts do not want their guests to leave too early so they delay feeding them as long as possible!

Guests can expect to be treated to a variety of tasty dishes, such as roast chicken, rice and beans, and occasionally sancocho (san-KOH-choh). Sancocho is a meat stew that

is served on special occasions. It includes up to seven different types of meat and uses starchy vegetables, such as potatoes, yams, and unripe plantains. Sancocho is flavored with fresh coriander, lemon, and spicy chili sauce and is served with white rice.

Since the hosts would want to be with their guests, those who can afford it will often have their parties catered so that the food arrives piping hot. When that is impractical or too expensive, the hostess and her closest female friends or relatives will supervise food preparation and serving.

specially prepared Dominican staples such as rice and beans, but might also include meat or fish, and *sancocho*.

EASTER The Easter meal is based on fish, typically fresh or cured codfish, served with potatoes.

CHRISTMAS The main dish of the Dominican Christmas meal is *lechón asado* (lay-CHON ah-SAH-doh), or roasted pig; the younger the pig, the more tender and flavorful. *Lechón asado* is served with rice cooked with beans or pigeon peas. The meal might

Traditional clay stoves are often used in rural areas.

also include turkey or chicken, and cassava, spaghetti, or fresh green salad. Traditionally, Dominican families raised their own Christmas pig, carefully feeding it all year in preparation for the holiday. Another traditional Christmas custom that has declined in recent years is eating boiled chestnuts.

IN THE KITCHEN

As increasing numbers of women seek employment as domestic servants to escape high rates of unemployment, more and more families find it possible to hire domestic help. Many middle- and upper-class families hire at least one maid to help cook, clean, and do laundry. The maid might either live in the house or come to work only during the day.

Dominican kitchens in the cities are usually equipped with modern electric stoves and refrigerators. In contrast, since many rural areas have no electricity, mothers cook the meals in a clay oven called a *fogón* (fo-GOHN), which is heated with a wood fire. These women must also walk to the nearest river or stream to fetch their water, which they ration carefully throughout the day for their cooking and cleaning purposes.

Open sacks
of beans are
presented at a
food market in
Santo Domingo.

MARKETS

There are three types of marketplaces in the Dominican Republic: the traditional open-air market with row upon row of individual vendors in their stalls or with their wares spread out on blankets; the small-town *colmados*, which sell basic supplies; and the modern supermarket with refrigerated meat and well-stocked shelves.

The Mercado Modelo in Santo Domingo is an amplified version of the traditional marketplace. Crowded with close-set stalls displaying goods of astounding abundance and variety, the market offers tambourines, drums, woodcarvings, ceramics, jewelry, leather belts and saddles, wicker, pocket-books, cigars, sandals, mahogany rocking chairs, tape cassettes of merengue music, T-shirts, and even voodoo products. Vendors on the outer edges of the market sell fresh poultry, pork and goat, as well as a variety of local produce—cassava, plantains, corn, pineapple, passionfruit, papayas, guavas, bananas, carrots, tomatoes, and potatoes.

Dominicans love to bargain over prices and become disappointed or contemptuous if denied the opportunity. The standard procedure begins when the shopper asks, with feigned indifference, the price of a particular product. No matter what price the vendor quotes, the buyer expresses shocked disbelief and a sense of disappointment, then rallies with a lower offer. The vendor reacts to the offer with disgust or dismay and starts to put away the item while throwing out a slightly lower price than originally quoted. The buyer might either give in and pay the lower price or try to pressure the vendor to lower it even more by starting to walk away.

Small-town *colmados* sell basic supplies such as rice, oil, sugar, salt, and rum. A single vendor manages the store, and the goods are generally sold at a fixed price.

Only the larger cities and towns have modern supermarkets, where women from the middle and upper classes do their shopping. The supermarkets exemplify a more modern, but impersonal, convenience.

In the urban areas, women in the lower classes generally shop at the large general marketplace, with its individual vendors, for their finished products such as shoes and clothes. Wealthier women shop for clothes at more expensive, European-style boutiques.

INTERNET LINKS

www.buzzfeed.com/irisestrada/what-to-eat-drink-in-the-dominican-republic-ewjg#.crGr4vKMn
Forty-five things to eat and drink in the Dominican Republic, with great pictures

www.dominicancooking.com/1370-about-dominican-cooking.html
The site presents an origin and history of Dominican cooking.

BATIDA DE LECHOSA (PAPAYA MILKSHAKE)

Fruit shakes are refreshing treats in the Dominican Republic. They are made with other tropical fruits, but papaya is the most popular flavor. Evaporated milk is traditional, but you can substitute fresh milk or almond milk. The taste won't be the same, however.

3 cups (700 ml) fresh or frozen papaya, cut into chunks

4 cups (950 ml) evaporated milk (not condensed)

1 tsp vanilla (5 ml), or more, to taste

½–1 cup sugar (100–200 grams), or to taste (alternatively you can use one ripe banana in place of sugar)

2 ½ cups (550 ml) ice cubes

Place all ingredients in large blender. Blend until creamy. Taste and adjust sugar and vanilla if necessary. Serve immediately.

ASOPAO DE POLLO (DOMINICAN CHICKEN AND RICE)

This favorite dish is a cross between a soup and paella. Sometimes shrimp is added during the last ten minutes of cooking.

2 Tbsp (30 ml) vegetable oil

1 or 2 smoked pork chops, diced

1 tsp (5 ml) dried oregano

1 Tbsp (15 ml) adobo seasoning

1 Tbsp (15 ml) brown sugar

1 tsp (5 ml) kosher salt

3-pound whole chicken, quartered

3 cloves garlic, minced

1 bell pepper, chopped

1 large carrot, diced

12-ounce (350 ml) can tomato sauce

1 quart (1 liter) water

2 cups (380 g) long grain white rice

1 cup (150 g) frozen green peas

½ lime, juiced

1 tsp (5 ml) olive oil

1 Tbsp (15 g) unsalted butter

Heat oil in a large stock pot and add diced pork chop. Remove from pot. Season chicken with oregano, adobo, sugar, and salt. Brown chicken parts in same pan. Add a little water and cover and cook for about 10 minutes.

Add garlic, peppers, and carrots and sauté gently for 5 minutes.

Add tomato sauce, rice, peas, and lime juice.

Cook uncovered for about 20 more minutes, stirring occasionally, until rice is plump and tender, and chicken is cooked through. (Add more water if necessary.) Consistency should be that of a thick soup. Before serving, stir in olive oil and butter.

Serve topped with fresh cilantro and avocado slices. Serves 6—8.

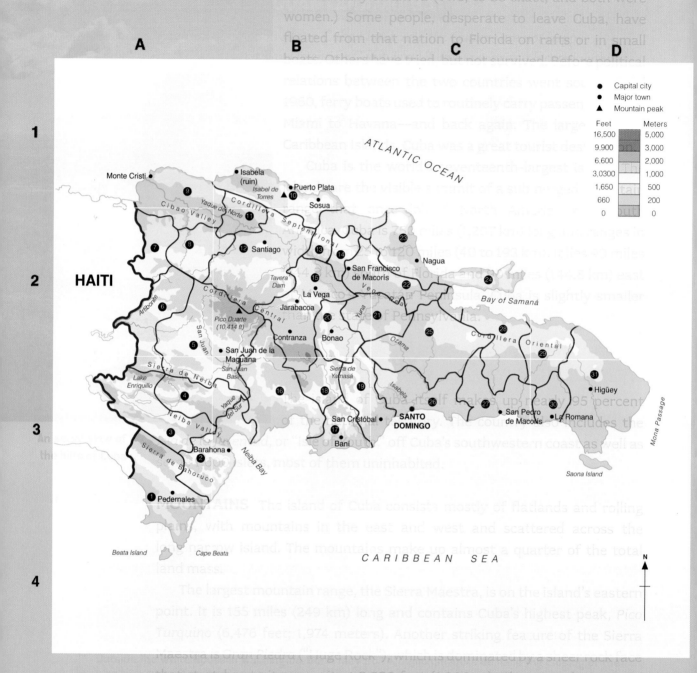

MAP OF DOMINICAN REPUBLIC

Artibonite, A2
Atlantic Ocean, A1, B1, B2, C1, C2, D1, D2
Azua, B2, B3

Bahoruco, A3, B3
Bani, B3
Barahona, A3, B3
Barahona (city), B3
Bay of Samaná, C2, D2
Beata Island, A4
Bonao, B2

Cape Beata, A4, B4
Caribbean Sea, A3—D3, A4—D4
Cibao Valley, A1, A2, B1, B2
Cordillera Central, A2, B2, B3
Cordillera Oriental, C2, D2, D3
Cordillera Septentrio-nal, A1, B1, B2, C2

Dajabón, A2
Duarte, B2, C2

El Seibo, D2, D3
Elías Piña, A2, A3
Espaillat, B2, C2

Haiti, A1, A3
Hato Mayor, C2, C3

Higüey, D3

Independencia, A3, B3
Isabela (ruin), B1
Isabela, C3
Isabel de Torres, B1

Jarabacoa, B2

La Altagracia, D2, D3
Lake Enriquillo, A3
La Romana, D3
La Vega (city), B2
La Vega, B2, B3

María Trinidad Sánchez, C2
Mona Passage, D3
Monseñor Nouel, B2, B3
Monte Cristi, A1, A2, B1, B2
Monte Cristi (city), A1
Monte Plata, B2, C2, C3

Nagua, C2
Neiba Bay, B3
Neiba Valley, A3, B3

Ozama, C2, C3

Pedernales, A3, A4
Peravia, B3

Pico Duarte, B2
Puerto Plata (city), B1
Puerto Plata, B1, B2

Salcedo, B2
Samaná, C2
Sánchez Ramírez, B2, C2
San Cristóbal, B2, B3, C3
San Cristóbal (city), C3
San Francisco de Macoris, B2
San José de Ocoa, B2, B3
San Juan, A2, A3, B2, B3
San Juan Basin, B3
San Juan de la Maguana, B2
San Juan River, A2, B3
San Pedro de Macoris (city), C3

San Pedro de Macoris, C2, C3, D3
Santiago (city), B2
Santiago, A2, B2
Santiago Rodríguez, A2, B2
Santo Domingo, C3
Saona Island, D3
Sierra de Bahoruco, A3, B3
Sierra de Neiba, A3, B3
Sierra de Yamasá, B2, B3
Sosua, B1

Tavera Dam, B2

Valverde, B1, B2
Vega Real, B2, C2

Yaque del Norte, A1, A2, B2
Yaque del Sur, B3
Yuna, B2, C2

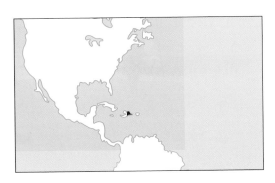

ECONOMIC DOMINICAN REPUBLIC

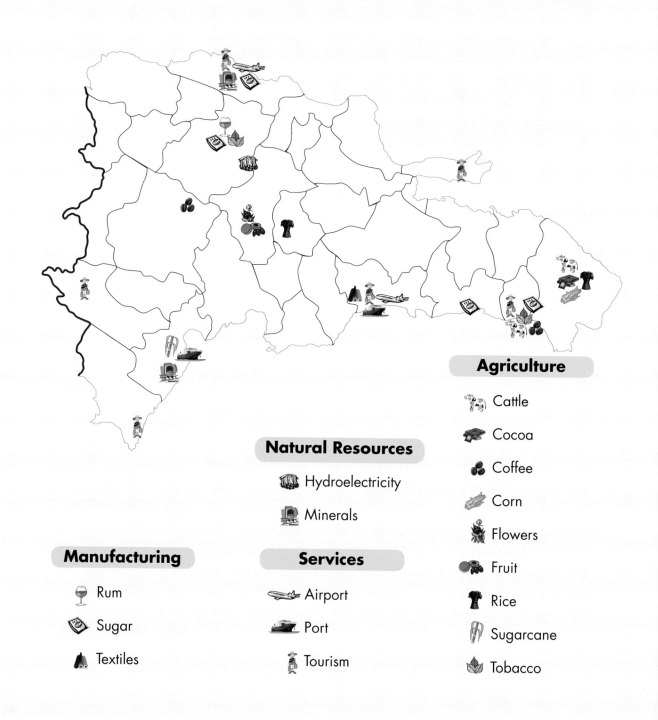

Agriculture

- Cattle
- Cocoa
- Coffee
- Corn
- Flowers
- Fruit
- Rice
- Sugarcane
- Tobacco

Natural Resources

- Hydroelectricity
- Minerals

Manufacturing

- Rum
- Sugar
- Textiles

Services

- Airport
- Port
- Tourism

ABOUT THE ECONOMY

OVERVIEW

The Dominican economy has been shifting from an agricultural to a service orientation since the 1980s. The country has had some of the highest growth rates in the region, especially in tourism, but Dominicans now have to deal with wide wealth gaps.

GROSS DOMESTIC PRODUCT (GDP)

$138 billion (2014)
Per capita $13,000 (2014)

GDP BY SECTOR

Agriculture 6.3 percent, industry 32.1 percent, services 64.7 percent (2014)

LAND USE

Arable land 16.6 percent, permanent crops 10.1 percent, other 73.3 percent (2011)

NATURAL RESOURCES

Nickel, bauxite, gold, silver

CURRENCY

1 Dominican peso (DOP) = 100 centavos
Notes: 5, 10, 20, 50, 100, 500, and 1000 pesos
Coins: 1, 5, 10, 25, 50 centavos; 1 peso
USD 1 = DOP 43.3 (2014)

AGRICULTURAL PRODUCTS

Sugarcane, coffee, cotton, cocoa, tobacco, rice, beans, potatoes, corn, bananas; cattle, dairy products, eggs

INDUSTRIAL PRODUCTS

Sugar processing, ferronickel and gold mining, textiles, cement, tobacco

INFLATION RATE

3 percent (2014)

WORKFORCE

4.996 million (2014); agriculture 14.4 percent, industry 20.8 percent, services and government 64.7 percent (2014)

UNEMPLOYMENT RATE

6.4 percent (2014)

MAJOR EXPORTS

Ferronickel, sugar, gold, silver, coffee, cocoa, tobacco, meats, consumer goods

MAJOR IMPORTS

Food products, petroleum, cotton and fabrics, chemicals and pharmaceuticals

MAJOR TRADE PARTNERS

United States, Canada, Haiti, Venezuela, Mexico, Colombia (2014)

MAJOR PORTS

Barahona, La Romana, Manzanillo, Puerto Plata, San Pedro de Macorís, Santo Domingo

CULTURAL DOMINICAN REPUBLIC

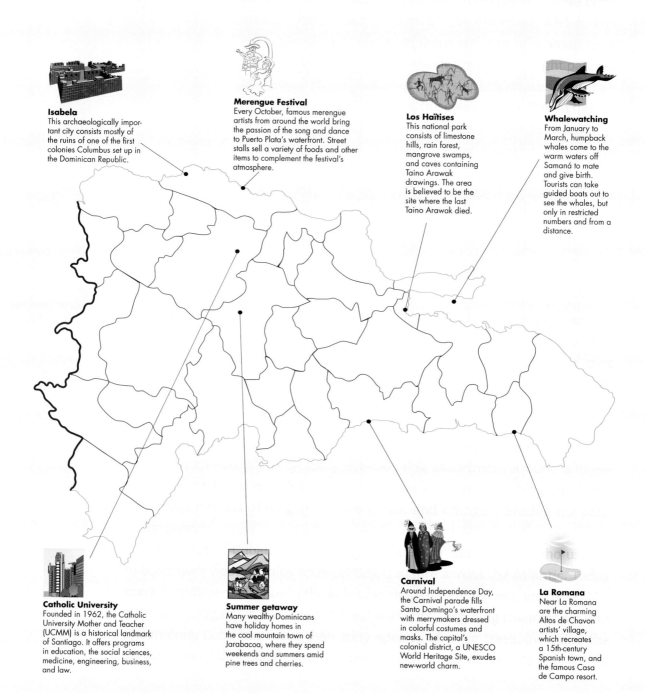

Isabela
This archaeologically important city consists mostly of the ruins of one of the first colonies Columbus set up in the Dominican Republic.

Merengue Festival
Every October, famous merengue artists from around the world bring the passion of the song and dance to Puerto Plata's waterfront. Street stalls sell a variety of foods and other items to complement the festival's atmosphere.

Los Haïtises
This national park consists of limestone hills, rain forest, mangrove swamps, and caves containing Taino Arawak drawings. The area is believed to be the site where the last Taino Arawak died.

Whalewatching
From January to March, humpback whales come to the warm waters off Samaná to mate and give birth. Tourists can take guided boats out to see the whales, but only in restricted numbers and from a distance.

Catholic University
Founded in 1962, the Catholic University Mother and Teacher (UCMM) is a historical landmark of Santiago. It offers programs in education, the social sciences, medicine, engineering, business, and law.

Summer getaway
Many wealthy Dominicans have holiday homes in the cool mountain town of Jarabacoa, where they spend weekends and summers amid pine trees and cherries.

Carnival
Around Independence Day, the Carnival parade fills Santo Domingo's waterfront with merrymakers dressed in colorful costumes and masks. The capital's colonial district, a UNESCO World Heritage Site, exudes new-world charm.

La Romana
Near La Romana are the charming Altos de Chavon artists' village, which recreates a 15th-century Spanish town, and the famous Casa de Campo resort.

ABOUT THE CULTURE

OFFICIAL NAME
Dominican Republic

CAPITAL
Santo Domingo

OTHER MAJOR CITIES
Santiago, San Pedro de Macorís, La Romana

GOVERNMENT
Representative democracy

COUNTRY FLAG
Segmented by a white cross into four rectangles, two blue and two red. In the center of the cross is a coat of arms: a shield supported by an olive branch and a palm branch. Above the shield is a blue ribbon with the words *Dios, Patria, Libertad* (God, Fatherland, Liberty), and below the shield is a red ribbon with the country's name.

NATIONAL ANTHEM
Quisqueyanos valientes (Valiant Sons of Quisqueye)

POPULATION
10,478,756 (2015)

LIFE EXPECTANCY
77.97 years; men 75.76 years, women 80,28 years (2015)

LITERACY RATE
91.8 percent (2015)

ETHNIC GROUPS
White 16 percent, black 11 percent, mixed 73 percent

RELIGIONS
Roman Catholicism 95 percent, Protestantism and others 5 percent

OFFICIAL LANGUAGE
Spanish

NATIONAL HOLIDAYS
New Year's Day (January 1), Epiphany (January 6), Our Lady of Altagracia (January 21), Duarte's Birthday (January 26), Independence Day (February 27), Carnival (variable), Good Friday (variable), Labor Day (May 1), Corpus Christi (variable), Restoration Day (August 16), Our Lady of Las Mercedes (September 24), Constitution Day (November 6), Christmas Day (December 25)

LEADERS IN POLITICS
Joaquín Balaguer Ricardo—president (1966–1978, 1986–1996)
Leonel Fernández Reyna—president (1996–2004);
Danilo Medina Sanchez—elected in 2012

TIMELINE

IN DOMINICAN REPUBLIC	IN THE WORLD
5000–4000 BCE First humans migrate from Central America.	
	753 BCE Rome is founded.
200 CE Arawak migrate from the Caribbean.	**116–117 CE** The Roman Empire reaches its greatest extent, under Emperor Trajan.
	600 CE Height of Mayan civilization
	1000 The Chinese perfect gunpowder and begin to use it in warfare.
1492 Christopher Columbus arrives.	
1496 Santo Domingo becomes the first Spanish colony in the Western Hemisphere.	**1530** Beginning of trans-Atlantic slave trade organized by the Portuguese in Africa.
	1558–1603 Reign of Elizabeth I of England
	1620 Pilgrims sail the *Mayflower* to America.
1697 Treaty gives western Hispaniola to France and eastern part to Spain.	**1776** US Declaration of Independence
1795 Spain cedes eastern Hispaniola to France.	**1789–99** The French Revolution
1808 Spain retakes eastern Hispaniola.	
1822 Haitian president Jean-Pierre Boyer annexes eastern Hispaniola.	
1844 First Dominican Republic proclaimed	
1861 Return to Spanish rule	**1861** The US Civil War begins.
1865 Spain withdraws.	**1869** The Suez Canal is opened.
1906 Fifty-year treaty with the United States	**1914** World War I begins.
1916–24 US occupation	

138 Cuba

IN DOMINICAN REPUBLIC	IN THE WORLD
1930	
General Rafael Leonidas Trujillo Molina establishes dictatorship.	**1939** World War II begins.
	1945 World War II ends.
	1957 The Russians launch *Sputnik*.
1961 Trujillo is assassinated.	
1962 Juan Bosch becomes president in first free elections in nearly four decades.	
1966 Joaquin Balaguer, Trujillo's designated successor, is elected president.	**1966–1969** The Chinese Cultural Revolution
1986, 1990, 1994 Balaguer is reelected president.	**1986** Nuclear power disaster at Chernobyl in Ukraine
	1991 Break-up of the Soviet Union
1996 Leonel Fernandez Reyna is elected president.	**1997** Hong Kong is returned to China.
1998 Hurricane Georges devastates the republic.	
2000 Hipolito Mejia is elected president.	
2002 Balaguer dies.	**2001** Terrorists crash planes in New York, Washington, DC, and Pennsylvania.
2003 High prices and power cuts lead to protests.	**2003** War in Iraq
2004 Leonel Fernandez is re-elected president.	**2004** Tsunami devastates Asia
	2009 Barack Obama becomes US president
	2010 Earthquake devastates Haiti
2012 Danilo Medina Sanchez elected president.	
2015 Supreme Court of Justice rules against Haitian immigrants in the Dominican Republic.	**2015** Rise of Isis in the Middle East

GLOSSARY

bateyes (bah-TAY-ays)
Caneworker settlements. Inhumane conditions in these settlements have provoked protests over human rights abuses.

bohíos (boh-EE-ohs)
Huts in which permanent agricultural workers live on company land.

cacique
The chief of a Taino Arawak village.

campesino
A farmer or peasant.

caudillo
A military dictator.

ceiba
The silk cotton tree.

colono (koh-LOH-no)
A small, independent sugarcane grower.

comida criolla (koh-MEE-dah kree-OH-yah)
The name for Dominican cuisine.

compadrazgo (kom-pah-DRAHZ-goh)
A system of godparentage.

dicho (DEE-choh)
A saying or expression.

fucú (foo-KU)
A sign that is likely to bring bad luck.

la novena (la noh-BAY-nah)
Nine consecutive days of prayers.

merengue
A style of music and dance believed to have originated in the Dominican Republic, or Haiti.

minifundios (mee-nee-FOON-dyos)
Small landholdings, the most common form of agricultural holdings in the Dominican Republic.

quinciñera (keen-see-NYAY-rah)
The fifteenth birthday celebration of girls from wealthy Dominican families.

tostones (tohs-TOHN-ays)
A popular snack of fried green plantains.

Voodoo
A religion practiced by Haitians in the Dominican Republic. It combines African animist beliefs and Roman Catholic rituals.

yolas (YOH-lahs)
Open boats used by illegal Dominican migrants to Puerto Rico.

FOR FURTHER INFORMATION

BOOKS

Alvarez, Julia. *Before We Were Free*. New York: Laurel Leaf Books, 2004.

Alvarez, Julia. *In the Time of the Butterflies*. Chapel Hill, NC: Duke University Press, 2010.

Aronson, Mark and Budhos, Marina. *Sugar Changed the World: A Story of Magic, Spice, Slavery, Freedom, and Science.* New York: Clarion Books, 2010.

Bedggood, Ginnie and Ilana Benad. *Dominican Republic - Culture Smart!: The Essential Guide to Customs & Culture*. London: Bravo Ltd., 2010.

Derby, Paul, Raymundo Gonzalez and Paul Roorda (eds.), *The Dominican Republic Reader*. Chapel Hill, NC: Duke University Press, 2014.

Klein, Alan, *Dominican Baseball: New Pride, Old Prejudice*. Philadelphia: Temple University Press, 2014.

DVDS/FILMS

Batey Mosquito. directed by Carmen Ballve, Eduardo Miyar. Hodge Podge Productions, 2008.

"Haiti and Dominican Republic: An Island Divided." Part 1 of series. *Black in Latin America*, with Henry Louis Gates, Jr. Directed by Ricardo Pollack. PBS, 2011.

In the Time of the Butterflies. Directed by Mariano Barroso. Metro-Goldwyn-Meyer, 2004.

Say Parsley (Di Perejil). Directed by Irene Rial Bou. CreateSpace, 2011.

MUSIC

Merengues from the Dominican Republic. Verna Gillis, 2015.

Musica Dominica 2015, Various Artists, 2015.

Putumayo Presents: República Dominicana. Various artists. Putumayo World Music, 2000.

Salsa Dominica, Various Artists, 2015.

WEBSITES

BBC News Country Profiles: Dominican Republic. news.bbc.co.uk/1/hi/world/americas/country_profiles/1216926.stm

Central Intelligence Agency World Factbook. www.cia.gov/library/publications/the-world-factbook/geos/dr.html

Embassy of the Dominican Republic in the United States. www.domrep.org

Library of Congress: Federal Research Division: Country. countrystudies.us/dominican-republic

US Department of State report on human rights in the Dominican Republic. www.state.gov/g/drl/rls/hrrpt/2004/41758.htm

BIBLIOGRAPHY

American Cetacean Society, "Humpback Whale." acsonline.org/fact-sheets/humpback-whale

BBC News Country Profiles: Dominican Republic.
news.bbc.co.uk/1/hi/world/americas/country_profiles/1216926.stm

Black, Jan Knippers. *The Dominican Republic: Politics and Development in an Unsovereign State.* Boulder, CO: Westview Press, 1986.

CIA World Factbook: Dominican Republic. www.cia.gov/cia/publications/factbook/geos/dr.html

Embassy of the Dominican Republic in the United States. www.domrep.org

FAO Country Profiles. www.fao.org/countryprofiles/index/en/?iso3=DOM

Haggerty, Richard A. *Dominican Republic and Haiti: Country Studies.* Washington, DC: Federal Research Division, Library of Congress, 1991.

Haverstock, Nathan A. (editor). *Dominican Republic: In Pictures.* Minneapolis, MN: Lerner Publications, 1988.

Jacobs, Francine and Patrick Collins (illustrator). *The Tainos: The People Who Welcomed Columbus.* New York: G.P. Putnam's Sons, 1992.

Klein, Alan. *Sugarball: The American Game, the Dominican Dream.* New Haven, CT: Yale University Press, 1991.

Library of Congress: Federal Research Division: Country. countrystudies.us/dominican-republic

Mintz, Sidney and Sally Price. *Caribbean Contours.* Baltimore, MD: Johns Hopkins Press, Ltd., 1985.

New York Times, The, Times Topics, Dominican Republic. topics.nytimes.com/top/news/international/countriesandterritories/dominicanrepublic/index.html

Organization for Economic Cooperation and Development. www.oecd.org

US Department of State report on human rights in the Dominican Republic. www.state.gov/g/drl/rls/hrrpt/2004/41758.htm

World Bank, The. www.worldbank.org/en/country/dominicanrepublic